THE COOPERATING TEACHER

A Practical Approach for the Supervision of Student Teachers

Pamela M. Balch
Patrick E. Balch

UNIVERSITY
PRESS OF
AMERICA

Lanham • New York • London

Copyright © 1987 by

University Press of America,® Inc.

4720 Boston Way
Lanham, MD 20706

3 Henrietta Street
London WC2E 8LU England

Printed in the United States of America

British Cataloging in Publication Information Available

Library of Congress Cataloging-in-Publication Data

Balch, Pamela M., 1950-
   The cooperating teacher.

   Includes bibliographies and index.
   1. Supervision of student teachers—United States.
2. Student teachers—United States.   3. Student teaching
—United States.   I. Balch, Patrick E., 1932]
II. Title.
LB2157.U5B24   1987   370'.7'33   87-10585
ISBN 0-8191-6424-0 (alk. paper)
ISBN 0-8191-6425-9 (pbk. : alk. paper)

All University Press of America books are produced on acid-free
paper which exceeds the minimum standards set by the National
Historical Publication and Records Commission.

Acknowledgements

We would like to express appreciation to Mrs. Nancy Martin, a certified math and science secondary education teacher from Elkins, W. V. for her sample student teacher handbook cited in Appendix C. Acknowledgements are extended to Diane Sirk of Advertising America in Morgantown, W. V. for her excellent artwork. We thank our two administrations (West Virginia Wesleyan College and West Virginia University) for granting our sabbaticals to allow time to research background data for this text. Gratitude is offered to the many public school teachers and university faculty who studied rough drafts and provided suggestions for improvement.

A special word of "thank you" is extended to our two children, Paul and Julie, for enduring long periods of "computer time" while textbook work was in progress and while deadlines were being met. Thanks to both of you!

Table of Contents

vii

Preface

Most educators will agree that the influence of cooperating teachers on the preparation of student teachers is quite instrumental. Unfortunately, many researchers indicate that much of supervision experience actually is rated negatively as an influence on teaching effectiveness. Many student teachers become more rigid and authoritarian, more conservative with less flexibility, and less responsive to meeting individual student needs by the end of the student teaching experience.

This disappointing outcome is only minimally the result of ineffective or poorly chosen cooperating teachers. It is unusual for cooperating teachers to have received much guidance in leadership for these supervisory tasks. Little attention has been given to those competencies deemed essential for effective supervision. In fact, only two states even require any official form of certification for cooperating teachers.

This book therefore has been designed as a practical aid for classroom teachers and administrators who may have the opportunity to work with student teachers. The book may be utilized for university or college courses designed for supervision of student teachers, as a reference guide for elementary or secondary classroom teachers and principals, or for use in inservice and preservice workshops dealing with supervision.

The authors have minimized attention to theories of supervision and have maximized the practicalities. The "how to's," and "when to's" are provided with the confidence that they will work to help teacher education candidates to become reasonably aware, sensitive, prepared, and knowledgeable classroom teachers. The authors encourage cooperating teachers to utilize many of the techniques presented. Each suggestion has potential for improving the teaching/learning environment necessary for successful supervision.

We also would like to point out that throughout the text we have chosen specific, but randomly used pronouns such as he, him, she, her, etc. when referring to a teacher or student teacher. We recognize the importance and the major numbers of female instructors, but our choice to vary the pronouns was made to lend a more human quality which can be destroyed by a she/he in each instance as a means of achieving equality.

The major learning objectives of this book are directed to provide necessary aid to the cooperating teacher to help the student teacher to develop the following cognitive and affective behaviors: 1) making decisions, 2) applying theory to practice, and 3) developing professional attitudes. We wish you success with this text and hope that it will help you to feel more competent, confident, and pleased with your role as a cooperating teacher.

Each chapter includes open-ended questions at the beginning which are designed to encourage curiosity, promote thought, and stimulate interest in the search for answers. It is suggested that you promote interest in discovering answers to the questions by group discussion.

Realistic problem situations (Problem Analyses) are added to enhance self-analysis, consider various evaluation strategies, and allow for class debate and discussion. The authors seldom offer the "right answers" in an attempt to encourage divergent thinking and decision making on the part of each student in your class.

At the conclusion of each chapter is a section entitled "Applying Ideas." These suggested assignments or projects may be given as applied research homework or as classroom activities. For example an important assignment for cooperating teachers, the development of a student teacher handbook, is given in Chapter Four under "Applying Ideas."

The authors have attempted to stimulate classroom discussions and sharing sessions through the format of the book. There is a great deal of room left for flexibility and creativity as you design activities for cooperating teachers.

THE COOPERATING TEACHER: A PRACTICAL APPROACH FOR THE SUPERVISION OF STUDENT TEACHERS

"I REALLY LIKE THE SOUND OF IT!"

Orienting Inquiry:

1. How important is the cooperating teacher to the student teacher? to the college teacher education program? to the profession?

2. What criteria are used to select cooperating teachers?

3. List several advantages of accepting and working with a student teacher.

4. List possible disadvantages with having a student teacher.

DECISIONS • DECISIONS • DECISIONS •

LEGAL PROBLEMS?

CONFLICT?

WHAT HAPPENS TO MY STUDENTS?

AM I A TEAM TEACHER?

WHO NEEDS IT?

COMMITMENT?

PERSONALITIES?

CLASS CONTROL?

"IS IT FOR ME?"

"Emerson advised his fellow
townsmen to manufacture school teachers
and make them the best in the world."
Van Wyck Brooks (1)

Researchers in the area of teacher education
indicate clearly that of all the persons in the
teaching training program the cooperating teacher
has the greatest influence upon a student's
success or failure as a classroom teacher. Funk
and others (1982) found that 70 percent of the
student teachers ranked the cooperating teacher
as "most significant." The characteristics most
often mentioned for top teachers were
"supportive," "enthusiastic," "pleasant," and
"challenging." Second to cooperating teachers in
ranking for most signficant influence were peers
or relatives. (2) In a similar study in England
and Wales, Yates (1982) found that 72 percent of
student teachers felt that the cooperating
teacher was of greater help than the college
supervisor and 78 percent viewed the evaluation
of the cooperating teacher as being more valid
than the college supervisor. (3)

Given this responsibility and influence on a
future teacher, why would an elementary or
secondary teacher or administrator assume this
great task? Researchers have been curious to
find the answer to this question. They have
found that financial compensation and tangible
incentives from state departments, local
education agencies, and institutions of higher
education rated high as motivation. (4) Another
researcher studied variations in compensation
throughout the fifty states and reported that the
amount of compensation varied from no payment at
all to a tuition waiver worth $390.00. He
found many differences even within states.
However, most frequently the stipend was the
responsibility of the institution of higher
education. It was also of interest to note that
he found only small changes in compensation
during the preceding ten years. (5)

2

The second greatest motivation given for accepting a student teacher was the meaningful participation in the teacher education process. (6) In fact Stout, (1982), in his research with secondary teachers, reported that 73 percent identified an intrinsic responsibility for student teaching as a professional obligation as the most positive reason for accepting student teachers, while only five percent identified monetary rewards. (7)

Obviously cooperating teachers and administrators accept student teachers for varying reasons, but most include goals which allow students to explore teaching styles, apply the theory learned in colleges, acquire the skills necessary to individualize teaching, and to gain the confidence and independence needed to be a classroom teacher.

Accepting a student teacher is a big commitment. The implications have a life long impact on many young people. Alford (1983) helps to maintain perspective in the following quote: "The role of supervising teacher requires a commitment unlike that in any phase of teaching. Involving hours of patient preparation and weeks of tedious progression in classroom technique, student teacher-supervisor relationships are an investment in the education of tomorrow. Like financial investments, some of these experiences yield excellent interest while others result in what seems to be a deficit." (8)

How Are Cooperating Teachers Selected?

The initial identification of cooperating teachers poses difficult problems for the college placement person. In a study conducted throughout 36 states, Morris (1982) found that several sources were used to identify the cooperating teachers. The percentages given indicate the extent to which the participants in the study used the method suggested by each

3

source of information.

Data Source	Extent Used as Selector
Principal	88%
College Supervisor	82%
Central Office Personnel	67%
College Faculty	49%
Student Teachers	46%
Teachers Inquiring or Volunteering to become a cooperating teacher	34%

(9)

Finding the appropriate classroom setting and the best qualified cooperating teacher for the maximal professional growth of a specific student teacher is a nearly impossible task. Cocoran (1982) states that "for the most part it is the overall <u>quality</u> of a classroom that influences teacher educatators as they select the classroom setting in which to place their preservice teachers. Consideration of the relative degree of complexity from the preservice teacher's point of view seldom comes into play. Until educational researchers and practitioners begin to focus more directly on the classroom contexts in which preservice teachers are expected to learn how to teach, teacher education will continue to be plagued by unexamined factors which inhibit or prevent seemingly qualified preservice teachers placed in seemingly model classrooms from learning to teach." (10)

A cooperating teacher may be a superb role model, but in a particular classroom which contains wide ranges of individual differences, a student teacher may find it is impossible to feel the success necessary to build the self-confidence needed to become an independent teacher. The persons responsible for selecting field placements must consider the classroom contexts, including the activities and experiences available, in addition to the overall

4

competencies of the cooperating teacher.

Major Advantages and Disadvantages of Accepting a Student Teacher

Before the final commitment is made to accept a student teacher, a teacher or administrator must weigh several of the potential pros and cons of this responsibility.

Pros:

1. Probably the most convincing argument for accepting a student teacher is intrinsic. "Student teaching has remained nearly unscathed as a necessary, valuable, and vital part of a teacher education program." (11) Therefore, a cooperating teacher has tremendous and valuable input into this important part of the college education of a student teacher. Your role becomes an immeasurable addition to the teaching profession. Knowing that an excellent new teacher will be entering the profession because you put forth the extra effort is a benefit that can only be measured internally by the cooperating teacher.

2. The student teacher is a valuable source of creative ideas and new techniques which can benefit the children and stimulate you to follow suit.

3. Two teachers in the room allow for more individualized help for your students.

4. With the student teacher's assumption of greater teaching responsibility, you can prepare materials, plan conferences, and reflect upon the curriculum and methods while observing a new professional.

5. While the student teacher is instructing the class, you may observe the students and learning process from a different perspective, perhaps gaining additional insight into teaching and learning.

6. There is no stronger bond than the one that binds two professionals in the "give and take" of the student teaching experience. Many of those friendships are active for years.

Cons:

1. Teachers who accept student teachers should be concerned with the potential legal problems associated with this additional responsibility. In researching the extent of this concern, it is apparent that very few court cases have been instituted by student teachers. Most recent challenges to date focus not on substance of the evaluation, but on due process. (12) Apart from the usual risk of suits in tort for negligence, student teachers are generally not of sufficiently high stature to serve as defendants in suits by pupils or parents. (13) The cooperating teacher often is the buffer and peace maker when these difficulties involve the student teacher and the parents.

2. Cooperating teachers face the possibility of receiving and dealing with the "marginal" student teacher. It becomes difficult in cases such as these to draw the line between satisfactory and unsatisfactory performance in the classroom. The cooperating teacher's evaluation affects the potential professional success of the teacher candidate.

3. Established discipline and routine may be upset by procedures and methods of the student teacher. Purcell and Seiferth (1982) found that the item of greatest difficulty for student teachers was indeed the inherent discipline problems that accompany the beginning teacher's efforts as he learns how to manage groups. (14)

4. There is always a possibility of receiving a "problem" (not necessarily marginal) student teacher. Chapter 10 will elaborate on the types and offer suggestions for dealing with these particular individuals.

5. Finally, you are on call as the resident specialist, the role model, and as such you open

the door to criticism by the student teacher. The following comments have been mentioned at times by student teachers:

"I wish that you had told me about the laws and rights of students."

"I don't think that you ever really observed me carefully."

"I never knew how I was doing until my final evaluation."

"We never really felt comfortable sharing thoughts with each other."

"My teacher never trusted me with her students because she was always in the room when I taught."

Given both sides of the supervising question, there fortunately continues to be a number of adventuresome souls who are willing to supervise student teachers. They may reflect upon their own experiences and see a real need to improve the system. Teachers interviewed in the Harris Poll agree that they were "not prepared at all for the total classroom experience." Ninety percent of the teachers in the poll said that they favored requiring new graduates to serve guided apprenticeships before being certified as teachers. (15)

We therefore dedicate the remainder of this book to those teachers and administrators who volunteer a part of their professional effort to influence and prepare the young teacher to survive and excel and to help maintain the continuity of society that only quality education can guarantee.

CONTRIBUTION

INFLUENCE

RESPONSIBILITY

PRESTIGE

CHALLENGE

"I REALLY LIKE THE SOUND OF IT!"

PROBLEM ANALYSIS No. 1: WHO NEEDS A CHALLENGE?

Your friend, a colleague, has had a discomforting experience with a below average student teacher named Diane. Diane eventually withdrew in the last part of student teaching to "get herself together." You are aware of most of the problems because of your close association with your friend. You are therefore surprised when a college instructor asks if you would be willing to accept Diane as a student teacher for the next semester.

MAKING DECISIONS:

Should you refuse to accept Diane because the knowledge you have gained might bias future decisions? Should you accept Diane to give her a second chance to succeed? Should you involve your colleague and the college instructor in this debate and in your final decision?

PROBLEM ANALYSIS No. 2:   A   DESIRE   TO   HELP   IS REJECTED

You have completed a course on the supervision of student teachers and would like to work with student teachers. You know that you could help student teachers find success. Whenever a student teacher is assigned to your building, however, either Mrs. Zimmerman or Mr. Taylor gets the assignment. You have seen the effort that they extend and feel that at best it is minimal. You know that you could do a much more thorough job of supervising.

When you express your desire to receive a student teacher, the principal answers, "we usually only receive two student teachers a year and Mr. Taylor and Mrs. Zimmerman, as senior staff members, have always taken these assignments. I hesitate to disturb a successful system."

MAKING DECISIONS:

Do you accept the situation or try a different approach? Should you contact the college and make the same request?

PROBLEM   ANALYSIS   No.   3   "NEVER   SAY   NEVER"

You have considered both pros and cons of working with student teachers and have decided against the task. The major reason is that you do not want to work with a potential "problem student teacher" and inflict that kind of conflict into your class.

One day a student from the college stops by your school for an appointment with you. The student says, "I have heard that you are very creative and use exciting techniques. Everyone knows that your students enjoy you as a teacher. I would really appreciate it if you would allow me to student teach with you. I want to learn how to be the very best I can. Will you take me on as a student teacher?"

MAKING DECISIONS:

What do you tell the student? If someone seeks out your talents with that strong an appeal, is it your responsibility to help, to perhaps rethink your prior decision? How would you suggest any prospective teacher go about investigating the background of a potential student teacher?

PROBLEM ANALYSIS No. 4:   CAN A STUDENT TEACHER CHANGE THE ENVIRONMENT?

You feel that a student teacher may destroy your established classroom environment. You have a good rapport with your students and you are fearful that a student teacher will change this climate and influence the class in a negative way. You are apprehensive about accepting a student in your classroom.

MAKING DECISIONS:

How can a student teacher influence the rapport and the environment of a cooperating teacher's classroom? What safe-guards might you suggest that an apprehensive teacher might implement to maintain a stable environment?

Applying Ideas:

1. Take a survey of fellow teachers who have had student teachers. Ask them to categorize their student teachers into one of two groups, positive relationships or negative relationships. You may want to clarify as a group what might be meant by "negative." Combine all of the results into a total percentage. What do these results suggest about the cooperating teacher experience? Are these results usual or atypical?

2. Have all class members discuss their own student teaching experiences, both positive and negative. Have them allude to changes which they might make based on personal experience.

3. As a take home assignment, ask each student to list the behaviors of an A+ teacher. In the follow-up class session, compile the group's ideas and prioritize each quality. How would you develop these traits in a student teacher?

NOTES: CHAPTER ONE

1) Van Wyck Brooks. The Flowering of New England. Chapter 13.

2) Fanchon F. Funk, Bruce Long, Anne M. Keithley, and Jeffrey L. Hoffman. "The Cooperating Teacher as Most Significant Other: A Competent Humanist," Action in Teacher Education. Fall, 1982. v. 4 n. 2 57-64.

3) John W. Yates. "Student Teaching: Results of a Recent Study," Educational Research. June, 1982 v. 24, 212-215.

4) Charles R. Whaley and Delores M. Wolfe. "Creating Incentives for Cooperating Teachers," Journal of Teacher Education. July/August, 1984. v. 35 n. 3, pgs. 46-48.

5) D. Black. Cooperating Teacher Renumeration: Where Are We? Reston, Va.: Association of Teacher Educators, 1980.

6) Whaley and Wolfe, Ibid.

7) Candace Stout. "Why Cooperating Teachers Accept Students," Journal of Teacher Education. Nov./Dec., 1982,v. 33 n.6, 2-24.

8) H. Evelyn Alford. "Student Teachers: Tomorrow's Mirrors," Delta Kappa Gamma Bulletin. Spring, 1983, 49: 15-19.

9) John E. Morris, J. Donald Hawk, and Eldon Drake. "Most Frequently Used Methods and Criteria for Identifying, Selecting, and Continuing Supervising Teachers," The Teacher Educator Winter, 1981-1982. v. 17 n. 3 p. 15.

10) Ellen Corcoran. "Classroom Contexts as Settings for Learning to Teach: A New Direction for Research in Teacher Education," _Action in Teacher Education._ v. 4 n. 1 Spring/Summer, 1982, 52-55.

11) William A. Bennie. _Supervising Clinical Experiences in the Classroom._ New York: Harper and Row, 1972, p. 2.

12) Virginia Helm. "Defamation, Due Process, and Evaluating Clinical Experiences," _Action in Teacher Education._ Fall, 1982, v. 4 n.2, 27-32.

13) U. R. Hazard. _Student Teaching and the Law._ Washington, D.C.: ERIC, 1976, p. 2.

14) Thomas D. Purcell and Bernice B. Seiferth. "Tri-State Survey of Student Teachers," _College Student Journal,_ Spring, 1982, v. 16: 27-29.

15) Linda Chion-Kenney. "Teaching: It All Starts in Elementary School," _Education Week._ v. IV n. 1, Sept. 5, 1984 (p. 18-19).

Orienting Inquiry:

---

1. What is the function of a supervision model?

2. Why do you need a model for supervision?

3. What qualifications does one need to possess to be a "clinical" supervisor?

4. What components of a model like clinical supervision can I adapt?

5. What are the alternatives to clinical supervision?

> "Simply stated, supervision is a human enterprise which seeks to help teachers provide high quality classroom experiences for students."
> Thomas J. Sergiovanni (1982) (1)

The earliest teacher training institutions in the United States were the normal schools of the early 1800's. The concept underlying the teaching experience was one of apprenticeship: learning a trade from one who already possessed the skills of the trade. The objective was to produce teachers who taught in the same way as those who trained them.

By the 1950's the objective of teacher education became the study of the teaching act rather than the practice of specific techniques of instruction. Apprentices became student teachers and the "master" teacher took on a new role as the "supervising teacher." (2)

Increased attacks on teacher eduation in the 1960's by critics like Kozol, Holt, Goodman, Postman and Weingartner, Conant, Illich, and Koerner, helped to force teacher education programs to become more accountable. Supervision became more "clinical" and scientific in data collection and interpretation.

The Development of Clinical Experiences

A model known as "clinical supervision" was developed in the 1960's by Cogan, Goldhammer, and others at the Harvard School of Education. The procedure has also been labeled as "teacher-centered supervision," emphasizing the "person-centered counseling" theory popularized by Carl Rogers. (3)

Clinical Supervision Defined

Clinical supervision may be defined as supervision "focused upon the improvement of instruction, by means of systematic cycles of planning, observing, and intensive analysis of the actual teaching performances in the interest of rational modification." (4)

Although the literature on clinical supervision is diverse, there is general agreement on its major function—to improve field experiences for teachers. Clinical supervision requires a structured system of observing and conferring with teachers. (5)

Clinical supervision includes three basic components:

1) Planning conferences between the cooperating teacher and student teacher to discuss procedures and concerns, to explore new techniques, to decide upon types of observation data needed, and to design activities to relieve tensions;
2) Classroom observations in which data are collected (through direct and indirect observation). The suggested observation techniques (see chapter 6) serve to indicate the present quality of a teaching performance; and

16

3) <u>Feedback</u> <u>conferences</u> in which the cooperating teacher and student teacher evaluate and interpret the data, discuss strengths and weaknesses, and prepare conclusions and suggestions for the next planning conference. Thus, the planning, evaluating, and incorporation of data are cycled through the process many times in the student teaching session.

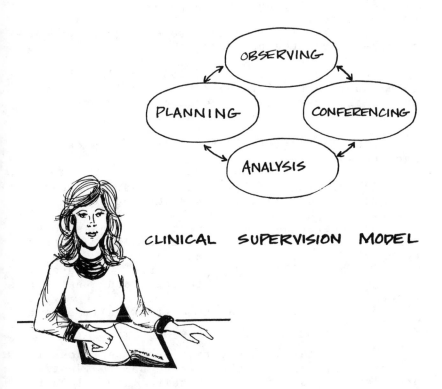

CLINICAL SUPERVISION MODEL

<u>Basic</u> <u>Components</u> <u>of</u> <u>Clinical</u> <u>Supervision</u>

An example of topics and activities of each component is provided so that you may plan the type of sessions with your student teacher which may be most productive to him. The planning or pre-observational conference may include such topics or strategies as:

1) developing rapport between the cooperating teacher and the student teacher.

17

2) establishing the purposes and function of classroom observations.

3) agreeing on the aspects of the instructional program that can be measured or observed.

4) developing procedures to be used during the observation phase.

5) identifying roles of cooperating and student teacher during the observation periods.

6) identifying the purposes of the follow-up conference.

7) answering student teacher questions or concerns about the process. (6)

The observation session should include techniques that will help to identify strengths and weaknesses. Ideas for specific observation techniques are provided in Chapter 6.

The conferencing or follow-up session may include such topics as:

1) viewing and listening to available data.

2) discussing the data collected during the observation phase.

3) answering student teacher questions, comments, or frustrations which may occur at this point.

4) analyzing strengths and weaknesses, first by the student teacher and then if necessary by you.

5) designing a plan to correct an immediate problem or concern.

The clinical supervision experience is directed at helping the new teacher to identify and clarify problems, to receive and classify data supplied by the supervisor, and to develop results. It is particularly effective if a three way meeting of the student teacher, cooperating teacher, and college supervisor can be arranged periodically.

Prior to the 1960's, the cooperating teacher played a major leadership role of recognizing needed changes and offering suggestions on how the changes should be made. In that setting he was responsible for the definition of efficient and effective instruction and served as the model

18

that the candidate attempted to imitate.

Conversely, clinical supervision attempts to involve the student teacher in the process to produce a "self-directed teacher." Research was conducted in 1980 to examine changes in teachers' behaviors who were trained in the clinical supervision model. It was found that teachers became more supportive in their work with others through this self-exploration and analysis aspect.(7)

Acheson and Gall outline five major goals of clinical supervision:
1) to provide the teacher with objective feedback concerning the current state of instruction.
2) to diagnose and solve instructional problems; to pinpoint discrepencies between what they are doing and what they ought to do;
3) to help the teacher to develop skill in using instructional strategies; to endure patterns of behavior in promoting learning, motivating students, and managing the classroom;
4) to evaluate the teacher; and
5) to help the teacher to develop a positive attitude and interest in continuous professional development. (8)

As in most situations, the interpersonal relationship that develops between the student teacher and cooperating teacher during a clinical type of supervision will influence all aspects of the teaching act. The more open, collaborative, and nondefensive the climate, the more the teachers will be satisfied with their supervision and feel that it is productive for them. (9)

Variations on the Clinical Supervision Theme

The clinical supervision model has great adaptability potential. Parts and pieces can be used in a variety of ways to improve instruction. The model can be shaped to fit the realities of flexible classroom needs. For example, peer supervision has become a plausible and effective type of learning process. Clinical supervision, particularly, lends itself to peer supervision because of its emphasis on the non-authoritarian relationship between teacher and supervisor. (10) As you will discover with use, many of the techniques can be implemented for self evaluation and self instruction to improve your own teaching activities.

Several institutions of higher education have experimented with peer teams of student teachers in the same classroom. The University of Oklahoma, for example, has a group team plan consisting of the cooperating teacher, the university supervisor, and two student teachers, all of whom share in all phases of student teaching. (11) Johnson (1982) in his study concerning communication patterns, found that the elementary and secondary majors who were placed in pairs, performed better than in single settings. Also, the student teachers who were grouped in pairs ranked their student teaching experience four points higher than those who were in a single placement group. (12) The peer interaction between student teachers may often benefit the observer as well as the teacher. Another variation can be seen in a program conducted by West Virginia University that has added an education and arts and sciences mentorship team to supervise and work with the classroom teacher for each candidate from one of the sciences. The paired team approaches should merit future examination and experimentation by cooperating teachers and university supervisors.

Goldsberry (1981) suggests that "the experiences of systematically observing one's colleagues, analyzing collected data, and structuring and conducting conferences may well contribute as much or more to the professional development of the observer as to the teacher being observed." (13) The process benefits both parties involved in the teaching and learning cycle.

Another variation described by Alfonso and Goldsberry (1982) includes an emphasis on the use of "colleague consultation." In this adaption of clinical supervision, the designers encourage the form of the model, but de-emphasize the reliance upon the analysis of methodology and instead utilize their colleagues' suggestions for teaching improvement. (14)

Richard Weller expands on the adaptable nature of clinical supervision in his statement that it can "range in practice over a broad continuum from nondirective to directive, supportive to high-pressured, and analytic to prescriptive." (15) If a teacher would like to use the concepts of clinical supervision, he can utilize the model to his situational needs.

An Evaluation of Clinical Supervision

"The majority of research on clinical supervision has been unsystematic, unrelated to other research, globally evaluative, and of very limited scope." (16) Many of the cooperating teachers who do utilize clinical supervision techniques often do not use the complete model. However, it is considered by many educators to fit the criterion of "best existing practice." A clear advantage of utilizing clinical supervision with the emphasis on analysis of observational data and the technique of joint comparison is that it increases the student teacher's ability to self-evaluate and to examine his own teaching patterns. (17)

Garman (1982) explains that clinical supervision consists of "both a focused problem-solving procedure involving identifying, collecting, and interpreting information explicitly germane to the educational goals accepted by teacher and supervisor, and a congruent and permeating spirit of personal commitment to growth through colleagueship and collaboration." (18) Thus far, no distinct study shows either traditional supervision or clinical supervision as truly superior, but, taken as a whole, the studies do affirm clinical supervision as a positive and beneficial model for the improvement of instruction. (19)

The overall purpose of the model is to improve supervision skills which help create confident, effective, and successful student teachers. If one accepts the full spirit of the clincial supervision model or merely implements

21

the portions that are directly applicable to a situation, he moves toward a concrete strategy for collecting and analyzing data. Sirois found that "the conditions imposed on both teachers and supervisors by the model of clinical supervision encourage greater verbal participation on the part of the teacher." (20) Thus, the student teacher becomes more aware of how he is performing and how his teaching behaviors are affecting learning. This effort to allow the student teacher to become self-aware and self-evaluative may be the most important indications of your role as a top-notch cooperating teacher.

PROBLEM ANALYSIS No. 5:   "THE CLINICAL MODEL: TOO STIFLING TO USE"

Veronica presents a dilemma in an early conference. She tells you that she has been trained in a clinical type model and realizes that she is obligated to carry out her student teaching in this manner. However, she requests that you and she participate in the model on paper only to fulfill the college requirements. Her rationale for this "skirting the task" is that she is an extremely creative person who teaches best in excitement of the spontaneous approach and she will be too stifled, perhaps to failure, if forced to conform to the structure and patterns of clinical supervision. She asks that you let her demonstrate her abilities before you make a final decision.

MAKING DECISIONS:

Should you grant Veronica's request or flatly refuse it as a "con job."? Are there compromises possible?

PROBLEM ANALYSIS No. 6: TWO STYLES OF SUPERVISION FRUSTRATE ONE STUDENT TEACHER

Terri, your new student teacher, has adapted well to the planning, observing, and conferencing components of clinical supervision. The three person team effort of Terri, you, and the college supervisor is successful and beneficial to Terri's analysis, planning, and implementation of lessons. Mr. Zinn, the principal, observes Terri one day. He knows "good teaching" when he sees it and is from the traditional "do it as I say" school of supervision. In his conference with Terri, he shares with her a list of changes that she needs to work on. He tells her that he will be back in a week to see if she has implemented his list of items. Terri is upset with this approach, feels quite threatened, and asks for your help.

MAKING DECISIONS:

Should you attempt to enlighten Mr. Zinn in the fine points of the clinical approach? Should you tell Terri to utilize the changes especially when Mr. Zinn is observing? Should you try to incorporate his list into the planning cycle just as you would the data from the observation techniques sessions? What do you think is the most professional approach?

PROBLEM ANALYSIS No. 7: AN UNBALANCED TEAM

The college supervisor has asked you to participate as a cooperating teacher for a pair of student teachers in your general science classes for a twelve week period. You have had several student teachers before, but never more than one at a time. You agree to accept Ralph and Tim. Both boys are friendly and appear eager to student teach.

The problem developed slowly but it appears that Ralph has all the confidence, capabilities, and leadership qualities. Tim is reserved and has little self-confidence. Their planning and teaching is being done together, but Ralph takes the leadership role in all phases and in general does the important work. The boys seem to be happy with these roles, but you are concerned that Tim is not gaining the experience or

24

confidence he needs.

MAKING DECISIONS:

Should you accept the situation and know that everything will be smooth for the remaining five weeks? If not, how would you modify the team approach? How would you explain the changes to the two male student teachers?

Applying Ideas:

1. Encourage two students to develop a simulation of a typical planning session under the guidelines of clinical supervision. Ask them to role play this planning session for the class to observe. Discuss the elements that related to clinical supervision.

2. Assign a short paper for a take home analysis to summarize the potential advantages and disadvantages that the clinical supervision model would have for each particular teacher.

3. Plan for a class discussion to assess the ways in which the components of clinical supervision could serve as self-instructional or self-evaluative learning for the cooperating teacher.

NOTES: CHAPTER 2

1) Thomas J. Sergiovanni (editor and chairperson). ASCD 1982 Yearbook Committee: Supervision of Teaching. Alexandria, Va., p. vii.

2) Colden Garland. Guiding Clinical Experiences in Teacher Education. New York: Longman, 1982, p. 33-34.

3) Keith A. Acheson and Meredith Damien Gall. Techniques in the Clinical Supervision of Teachers. New York: Longman, Inc., 1980, p. 8.

4) Richard H. Weller. Verbal Communication in Instructional Supervision. New York: Columbia Teachers' College Press, 1971, p. 15.

5) Lee F. Goldsberry. "The Realities of Clinical Supervision," Educational Leadership. April, 1984, p. 13.

6) Richard A. Gorton. "The Realities of Clinical Supervision," Educational Leadership. April, 1984, p. 13.

7) Jon Thorlacius. "Changes in Supervisory Behavior Resulting from Training in Clinical Supervision." Paper presented at American Educational Research Assoc., Boston, MA: 1980.

8) Acheson and Gall, Ibid., p. 13-14.

9) Arthur Blumberg. Supervisors and Teachers: A Private Cold War. 2nd ed., Berkeley, CA.: McCutchan Publ. Co., 1980, p. 276-279.

10) Charles A. Reavis. Teacher Improvement through Clinical Supervision. Bloomington, Ind.: Phi Delta Kappa Educational Foundation, 1978, p. 42-43.

11) Thomas Gallaher, Anthony Romano, Cherlyn Sunflower, Gene Shepherd. "A Three Role Group Clinical Supervision System for Student Teaching," Journal of Teacher Education. March/

April 1983. v. 34 n.1 p. 48-51.

12) William Johnson, C. Benjamin Cox, and George
Wood, "Communication Patterns and Topics of
Single and Paired Student Teachers," Action in
Teacher Education. Spring/Summer 1982, v. 4 n. 1
56-60.

13) Lee   Goldsberry. "College   Consultation:
Teacher   Collaboration   Toward   Performance
Improvement." Paper presented at   AREA, Los
Angeles, April, 1981.

14) Robert   J.   Alfonso and Lee Goldsberry.
"Colleagueship in Supervision," Supervision of
Teaching. Edited by   T.J.   Sergiovanni.
Alexandria, Va.: ASCD, 1982.

15) Weller, op.cit., p. 17

16) Weller, op. cit.,p. 20

17) Shirley McFaul and James Cooper. "Peer
Clinical Supervision: Theory vs. Reality,"
Educational Leadership. April, 1984, p. 6.

18) Noreen B. Garman. "The Clinical Approach to
Supervision." Chapter 3 in Supervision of
Teaching, the 1982 Yearbook of the Assoc. for
Supervision and Curriculum Development. Edited
by Thomas J. Sergiovanni. Alexandria, Va.:
ASCSD, 1982.

19) Reavis, op. cit., p. 45.

20) Harold Sirois. "The Effects of a Clinical
Model of Supervision, Teacher Types, Supervisor
Types, and Styles on Changes in Teacher and
Student   Attitude and   Behavior." Unpublished
doctoral dissertation. Univ. of Connecticut,
1978.

Orienting Inquiry:

1. What new responsibilities will I accept if I become a cooperating teacher?

2. What type of supervisory style is most appropriate for assuring success and confidence in a student teacher?

3. How should I spend my time while my student teacher is assuming the teaching role?

"Becoming aware of reality in the school gives the prospective teacher insight to initiate change or provide direction in issues confronting his success in teaching, and becomes the basis for prudent decisions and problem solving." (1)

Several questions regarding responsibilities may arise as you consider working with a student teacher. What is expected when one takes on the title of cooperating teacher? How many and what kinds of different roles will be required ? How much influence willI have on the career of a new teacher? Can I make him aware of the realities in a positive way?

Your responsibilities will include many important aspects that will have a definite impact on a student teacher. You will become a clinical specialist who collects and interprets data concerning teaching behavior and helps new teachers benefit from interpretation and evaluation, a peer professional and friend to a new teacher, and a model teacher. It is not an easy task to maintain balance and perspective for your own classes as well as for the development of a new professional.

There are many ways to describe the job of a cooperating teacher. Weller chooses to divide the roles of the cooperating teacher into three distinct categories. "The functions of the supervisor may be called 1) counseling, 2) teaching, and 3) training. These functions represent a multidimensional continuum: from emphasis on personal adjustment to emphasis on understanding instructional phenomena, to emphasis on specific teaching behaviors." (2)

Other researchers describe the major roles of the cooperating teacher to be an onsite supervisor, a resource person, a perennial critic, an always available helper,and a professional friend and confidant. During all this, the cooperating teacher also bears the legal and professional responsibiity for the class. He may delegate the teaching/learning functions and activities to the student teacher, but he must be sure to know what is going on at all times.

In the total picture the cooperating teacher must also identify teaching strengths and weaknesses and with data and intuition recognize the chance for success and improvement. He must decide occasionally against those persons who do not appear to belong in the teaching environment.

Success in each of the roles of counselor, teacher, and trainer is crucial to the efforts of a truly outstanding cooperating teacher. The teacher who can incorporate all of these facets into the function as role model will influence in a positive way the future of each student teacher with whom he works.

Roles and Responsibilities

There are eight major roles that a cooperating teacher should portray throughout a student teacher's experience. The significance and amount of time spent on each role will vary depending on the personality, strengths, and

30

weaknesses of each student teacher. These role
expectations include:

1. model teacher
2. observer
3. planner
4. evaluator
5. conferencer
6. counselor
7. professional peer
8. friend

1. A Model

Humans learn a great deal by watching,
listening, analyzing, and then imitating
behaviors. We therefore learn much about
teaching by observing different types of
teachers. We internalize successful strategies
and vow to disregard poor ideas or unsuccessful
methods. We have all had good and bad
experiences with various types of teaching

models. Your student teacher will rely on your wisdom, experience, and interactions in the classroom to help him to become a dynamic teacher.

In your role as a model teacher you may need to explain why you do certain actions. You will need to encourage your student teacher to observe your teaching, ask questions, and evaluate student response to your style. You may choose to:

--demonstrate various teaching techniques and creative ways of getting away from the "textbook teacher."

--explain diagnostic and evaluative devices which measure achievement in content, intellectual skills, and attitudes.

--display a sense of good behavioral management techniques with a sense of consistency and fairness toward all students.

--share successful ideas for teaching units, learning stations, creative lesson plans, or other materials.

You may want to examine various checklists used to identify the outstanding teacher, review leadership training manuals, re-evaluate your own teaching philosophy, review the year's curriculum, check over your responsibilities as outlined in your student teacher's handbook, and guarantee that you are organized in your preparations. Your student teacher (and perhaps the students) will be impressed by your effectiveness as you attempt to do your best. It is not easy to be "up" every day, but the challenge of helping someone to see successful teaching by modeling excellence is worth your effort.

2. An Observer

Your role as a competent observer is critical to the development of a student teacher. Although observation seems like it should be an obvious and easy task, cooperating teachers are criticized more severely in this responsibility than in their other roles with student teachers. Often the cooperating teacher is too casual and informal to be of direct help to the student

32

teacher.

You must be a scientifically accurate and persistent observer, collecting enough data to supply answers about effectiveness, clarity, purpose, etc. when the right questions are asked in a conference. You will need to be alert to details and to be prepared to offer suggestions for changes. Being a successful observer does not imply that you begin writing notes at 8:00 A.M. and continue until 3:00 P.M. You must learn to be a selective observer and to utilize a variety of techniques to strengthen the teaching/learning process. Chapter Six (Becoming an Effective Observer) includes seven specific types of observation processes to help you in this role. There is a positive correlation between efficient observation/communication and improved teaching. This observing role is one in which you will want to achieve maximum success.

3. A Planner

You might expect that your role in the planning process could be diminished because your student teacher will be doing much of the preparation for lessons. You might also assume that since he has had practice in developing lesson plans and units in college coursework that he should be well prepared in this task. Neither of these expectations generally occurs. Even if your student teacher has had excellent background in lesson planning he will not be comfortable in accuracy of timing for activities or in handling students with varying needs and abilities. You will need to help with the planning process in several ways. For example you may need to:

--inform the student teacher of long range content and process objectives in order for him to coordinate his work with your own semester's plans.
--supply the rationale and school philosophy and curriculum as guidelines for planning.
--share your yearly plans, outlines, and methods for weekly planning.
--help the student teacher plan for time management according to students' interests, attention spans, and abilities.

33

--evaluate in advance your student teacher's plans so that you know that he is well organized, that the material is appropriate for your students, and that it will be presented in the most creative and interesting manner.

A great deal of your time, especially at the beginning, will be spent in this dual planning process to allow for superior teaching and learning. More specific suggestions in cooperative and guided planning with your student teacher are provided in Chapter Five.

4. An Evaluator

Some of the most difficult, yet essential responsibilities that you will have as a cooperating teacher will be to assess competence, pinpoint weaknesses, suggest changes, analyze growth, and formalize all of these processes into a final recommendation, perhaps even a letter grade. Evaluation has many components, from an informal comment to a formal letter of recommendation.

Your role as an evaluator is an on-going process, aided by frequent communication of your assessments to your student teacher. You will need to encourage him to become independent through his success with self-evaluations and analyses. Spend time asking your student teacher for his perceptions of strengths, weaknesses, for his areas of self-confidence or uncertainties, and for his opinions of his progress.

There are various models and techniques for evaluating teaching/learning interactions in a non-threatening way. Chapter Eight includes specific pointers to help in your role as an effective evaluator.

5. A Conferencer

Your leadership role in organizing and participating in conferences is vital to a student teacher's perception of progress. You must be open and willing to share insightful and objective feedback concerning instruction. As a cooperating teacher you should be able to provide an appropriate environment and to establish a working relationship that can promote a positive attitude toward evaluation, constructive criticism, and analysis of strategies. No one enjoys hearing about shortcomings, yet it is your responsibility to diagnose problems, offer feedback, and present alternatives at the conference sessions. The key to being a successful conferencer is to be honest and open in the most positive and constructive way that you can. Encourage your student teacher to do most of the talking during the conference sessions while you become a concerned listener. Review the suggestions offered in Chapter Seven to help provide you with appropriate techniques in conferencing with student teachers.

6.) <u>A Counselor</u>

One of the most rewarding responsibilities that you will encounter is the development of a unique personal and professional relationship with your student teacher. In this capacity you will relieve anxieties, administer fatherly or motherly advice, and listen a great deal.

Starting with your very first meeting, you will find that the beginner usually exhibits anxieties and concerns about things you can't even predict. Student teachers are visably concerned with the development of a friendly personal relationship with the cooperating teacher. The student teacher must feel safe and secure and willing to take some intellectual risks in this relationship with you. This secure relationship must exist even before the challenge of teaching or directing the class.

Campbell and Williamson (3) have identified three ordered stages which student teachers pass through as they become responsible beginning teachers. The stages are concerns with 1) self, 2) teaching actions and student behavior, and 3) pupil learning. They suggest that many students do not seem to reach the third stage during student teaching. The first stage, concern with self, involves questions like "Can I do this?" or "What does my teacher think of me?". This stage embraces and calls for the counseling role of the cooperating teacher. It may be unproductive for the cooperating teacher to raise the issue of pupil learning if the student teacher is struggling with identity-related issues. The second stage considers the concern with teaching actions and students' behavior. The student teacher starts the sessions with excessive lesson plans, but faces the realities of discipline problems. "I've got this great experience ready for you but you are busy trying to test my authority." You, as the cooperating teacher, must exercise patience and add reassurance to help the student teacher to build self-confidence. The final stage, if growth continues to this extent, is concern with pupil learning. It is at this point that the cooperating teacher can ease up on the worries of being a counselor and move on to effective action with his other roles.

7. A Professional Peer

Always function as a professional colleague as you help the student teacher take over various functions of your day. The students should be prepared to extend the same respects and courtesies to the student teacher as they do you. Even with increased independence the student teacher should count on you to be there at the beginning of each session to offer support, know the plan for the lesson, and be capable of "stepping in and out" of the lesson as a member of a team without undermining the authority that you have delegated to your colleague.

Professionally and socially help your student teacher to meet the total faculty, the staff, the parents, and the community. To promote individual responsibility for personal and professional growth you will need to establish a risk-free environment and an outgoing and experimental attitude. Invite the use of student teacher initiated new ideas, a unit developed in college classes, or found in the professional literature, or a special approach for some individualized study guides, always with the understanding that you will help to change plans if the experiment seems ineffective or needs some support.

It is essential that you help the student teacher feel accepted and respected as a member of a professional team doing an important job. When evaluating or commenting, remember that your utterances are considered "in your best professional judgment," and therefore should be well thought through, accurate, and worthy. Appropriate praise and positive feedback should stand the same test, but support and positive encouragement should be generously applied.

The following comments are requests by student teachers which may help you to assume the professional peer team member role:

"Please give me some freedom to choose how and what I would like to teach."

"I really need you to support my authority."

"Can you allow me to handle and follow up on my own discipline problems, but still be available for advice if my techniques don't work?"

"Please volunteer information concerning professional organizations. What else can I do to become a professional educator?"

As a professional you must enforce the ethics required as a confidant and protector of your charge. Student teacher troubles are not "table talk" at the lunchroom with fellow teachers or parents. If a problem merits attention, call the college supervisor, but even then a three way conference with the student teacher is recommended. (Also see legal implications in Chapter 13.)

8. A Friend

The task of being a friend is not mandatory for a successful professional relationship as are the other seven roles. However, if you offer your friendship to your student teacher you will be providing comfort and security that may not exist without such a relationship. In this role try to become acquainted with the needs, interests, and abilities of your student teacher. Talk about issues unrelated to school. Your efforts as a friend may be contagious and may set an example for that student teacher when he becomes a cooperating teacher.

The role you serve as a friend will be as variable as the student teachers themselves. As a friend you are not "doing it all to make it easy" on the student teacher. Rather it is important to show caring as evidenced in statements like "I know that the stress is getting to you, especially Bert and Charlie, but let's get away for lunch and tell each other just how great everything else is going" or "Sorry to interrupt your unit, but we must use ten minutes for a small birthday party for you. The kids have some cards and I have a small cake. Happy Birthday new teacher!" Or "Let me take the reading session at 10:30 so you can observe Mr. Clark's management technique in his home economic class for boys. Keep notes so we can find out how he does it." These friendships often reduce the anxiety which is hindering optimum teaching.

Student teachers offer the following requests to help you to fulfill your role as a friend:

"Please be honest, natural, and open in our discussions."
"Be candid in discussing your own shortcomings or lack of success in ideas you have tried."
"Introduce me to other staff members, and make me feel at home."
"Give me the freedom to choose whether or not I want you in every class when I have assumed full responsibility."
"Gather students' reactions to my teaching and then pass them on to me."
"Give me confidence in myself."
"Let me know that you are available if I need help."

Supervisory Styles

Cooperating teachers who exemplify all of the responsibilities discussed above may vary in effectiveness as a supervisor of student teachers. The reason for this variety is reflected in supervisory styles and personality. It may help to learn what factors in style are most important to student teachers. In a recent study (4) student teachers were asked to list factors that identified their cooperating teacher as superior. The first and most important single factor concerned the supportive nature of the cooperating teacher. The second factor of importance was enthusiasm shown by the cooperating teacher. Third in importance was a pleasant attitude and personality. The fourth factor cited was the challenging approach to learning used by the cooperating teacher. These are not too tough for our "model teacher." If you work at being supportive, enthusiastic, pleasant, personable, and offer challenges, you will be a superior cooperating teacher and may make a big difference for a generation of student teachers.

Each supervisory style seems to be the product of a teacher's own teaching experiences, personality characteristics, the local school environment, and his unique philosophy about the teaching/learning phenomenon. Some styles are more favorable to the cooperating teacher role.

Two major categories of style divide teachers into either direct or indirect teachers. Flanders (5) identifies direct teaching styles as those which include lecturing, directing, and criticizing. Indirect styles include the strategies of accepting feelings, encouraging, acknowledging, and using student ideas. Blumberg (1980) (6) applies this concept of direct-indirect style to the behavioral styles of the cooperating teacher. He explains four types of supervisory styles:

A. The High Direct, High Indirect Cooperating Teacher who tends to tell information and criticize, but also asks questions and listens to the student teacher.

B. The High Direct, Low Indirect Cooperating Teacher who also tells and criticizes, but with little time for asking questions or listening to problems.

C. The Low Direct, High Indirect Cooperating Teacher who rarely tells or criticizes, but asks many questions and spends time analyzing ideas and feelings.

   D. The Low Direct, Low Indirect Cooperating Teacher who is basically passive, with little direction and little time for listening to problems and allows the student teacher to learn by a laissez-faire manner.

   There are advantages to varying styles of supervision, but certain types are better for creating specific positive results in student teachers than others. Which type of supervisory style sounds like it would elicit the highest ratings for productivity and favorable comment by student teachers? Which style do you feel that you exemplify?

   Researchers have found that the most productive combination was the supervisory style C (low direct, high indirect) with style A (high direct, high indirect) a close second. Style D (low direct and low indirect) had a much lower rating and style B (high direct, low indirect) came in last.

   What do you think accounts for these results? Can you think of examples of particular teachers who may fit these patterns?

   An analysis of Blumberg's results indicates that teachers or student teachers want to have input into the learning experience, and are willing to accept criticism and direction if they are given the opportunity to be heard and if they receive encouragement. This is significant information to internalize when analyzing your responsibilities as a cooperating teacher.

   It is also of importance to note that the desired style and needed cooperative teacher efforts may change on the part of the student teacher as he gains experience and more self-confidence. Copeland (7) found that the student teachers, as they gained experience, knowledge of classrooms, and self-confidence, desired an increase in the indirect supervisory style. To the cooperating teacher this means that you must have the flexibility to be both direct and indirect as the situation demands and as the student teacher becomes more secure.

Appropriate Use of Supervisory Time

How do cooperating teachers utilize their time while supervising student teachers? List several ways that a poor supervisor might spend his time while not in the teaching role. Likewise list some valuable services that a cooperating teacher could do during the same amount of time allowed. Answers given by cooperating teachers to this question are quite different from how teachers actually do spend this time. Cooperating teachers usually feel that they tend to spend the supervisory time planning lessons and thinking about new educational ideas. However, in a survey (8) of cooperating teachers, a researcher indicated that teachers really use their time to read professional materials, attend staff development sessions, and work more diligently on developing interpersonal relationships among students.

The time spent working directly with the student teacher also varies. We would recommend that you spend about one hour per day for feedback, evaluation sessions, and curriculum planning. This will of course differ with the stages of student teaching, topics covered and the need to confer, discuss, and confide.

Quality supervision requires daily planning, guidance, and evaluation. You will need to take the time necessary to write comments, evaluate plans, discuss the day's activities, and plan to meet long range objectives. It is also essential to spend some of this busy schedule to produce activities designed to reduce stress and maintain an equilibrium for the both of you. Few student teachers come prepared to handle stress or to cope with anxiety.

The many responsibilities of a cooperating teacher represent many complex tasks ranging from emotional to cognitive in nature. The challenge is recognizable indeed as well as difficult. The results of an effective cooperating teacher are very rewarding, however.

PROBLEM ANALYSIS No. 8: "MY STUDENT TEACHER IS OUT OF LINE!"

You are presenting a music lesson on how to determine the right key signature. You present a short-cut method which you feel students will pick up with ease. Melinda, your student teacher, interrupts and says, "You are terribly wrong because that doesn't always work. Later on the kids will see that the easy way isn't always the best way."

MAKING DECISIONS:

What do you do at this point while still directing the class? Later, when you get an opportunity to speak to Melinda, do you 1) give her "heck" for unprofessional behavior, 2) get the author of the method you used so that she can see that she was incorrect, 3) explain and describe appropriate roles for professional team teachers, or 4) take a position and proceed in a different manner than any listed above?

PROBLEM ANALYSIS No. 9: "THE COLLEGE SUPERVISOR IS NOT AVAILABLE"

Tom has a very defensive attitude. He has been at the school for three weeks and you are becoming annoyed because he insists you document each complaint or observation in writing and contact the college supervisor on each issue. The college supervisor has not made an appearance in your school and hasn't responded to notes you have sent. You have called his office and left messages for him to stop by your school, but you've received no response. You feel that it is important that you have his support on several procedures you are about to try with Tom.

MAKING DECISIONS:

Do you give up on the college supervisor and proceed with necessary steps alone? Do you go over supervisor's head and call on his superior for some help? What would be your responsibility in this situation? What would you do with regard to Tom?

PROBLEM ANALYSIS No. 10: "TO WHOM IT MAY CONCERN"

You know that as a cooperating teacher you will be asked to write letters of recommendations to school administrators where your student teacher has applied for employment. It is, therefore, disturbing when Andrea, a mediocre teacher candidate, completes her student teaching with you, receives a "C-" for her final assessment, and then asks you for such a letter. She was knowledgeable in content, but had great difficulty in relating to and working with students. She phones to ask if you would send a letter of reference for her. Before you respond, she asks, "please make it a good one because I really need the job!"

MAKING DECISIONS:

What do you tell Andrea? Can you stay in the middle of the fence and not state a definite answer to her question? Knowing that you will have to write a very average letter, should you explain that your recommendations will be similar to her final evaluation and necessarily refer to weaknesses in management? How do you handle this role in a post-student teaching situation?

PROBLEM ANALYSIS No. 11: HOW MUCH PERSONAL COUNSELING IS ENOUGH?

Jessica is a very emotional person who brings personal problems to her first meeting with you. She asks for your advice and you offer your best opinions, although few of the questions are related to education. You feel that if Jessica works out some of these problems she will concentrate on teaching concerns. However, as the time passes, Jessica brings more, not fewer, personal concerns. You feel a bit like "Dear Abby." You wonder if she will _ever_ move from self-concern to concern with pupil. learning. However, you hesitate to tell her that hers are low level concerns.

MAKING DECISIONS:

Do you express your anxiety over her self-indulgence? Do you continue in this counselor role and hope that Jessica's priorities will change? Do you suggest that she seek out a "certified" counselor? Just how much is "enough?"

PROBLEM ANALYSIS No. 12: "I DIDN'T MEAN FOR YOU TO EAT IT ALL!"

You have explained to Carrie that she is welcome to use your file of materials, lesson ideas, units, and earning packets for suggestions to help her prepare her lesson plans. The suggestion was accepted and Carrie is now utilizing all planning periods and observation times for duplicating your materials for her own personal file. You have spent years working on these materials and it is disturbing you that she is using everything in this manner.

When you ask her about this concern, she says that she'll probably be teaching in another state and therefore there should be no problem with doing the same lessons. Besides she says that she will give you credit for your help.

MAKING DECISIONS:

Do you insist that Carrie not duplicate your total files? How do you make her aware of the time required for observing and working with individual children? Is Carrie out of line or are you "stingy?"

Applying Ideas:

1. Discuss and select those tasks that a cooperating teacher can do to "go the extra mile" to be an outstanding supervisor.

2. Have all class members self-analyze their own styles of teaching to determine which of the four types they most closely might emulate for a student teacher. Cite specific examples to indicate why.

3. Design a pattern of doing concrete tasks which may allow you to vary your style of supervision.

NOTES: CHAPTER 3

1)   Janice Wendt.   "Professional Preparation: A
Process of Discovery," Quest. v. 35 n. 2, Fall,
1971, p. 7-8.

2)   Richard H. Weller. Verbal Communication in
Instructional Supervision. Teacher's College
Press, Teacher's College, Columbia University,
N.Y., 1971, p. 7-8.

3)   Lloyd P. Campbell and John A. Williamson.
"Supervising the Student Teacher: What is Really
Involved?" NASSP Bulletin, Oct. 1983, v. 67 p.
77-79.

4)   L. David Weller. "Essential Competencies for
Effective Supervision of Student Teachers,"
Education, Winter, 1983. 104: 213-218., p. 2-3.

5)   Ned Flanders and Edmund Amidon. "Interaction
Analysis as a Feedback System," Interaction
Analysis: Theory, Research, and Application.
Ed. by Edmund Amidon and John Hough. Reading,
MA: Addison-Wesley, 1967, p. 122-124.

6)   Arthur Blumberg. Supervisors and Teachers:
A Private Cold War. (2nd ed.) Berkeley, CA:
McCutchan, 1980, p. 66.

7)   Willis D. Copeland. "Student Teachers'
Preference for a Supervisory Approach," Journal
of Teacher Education. May/April, 1982. v. 33. 32-
36.

8)   Lloyd Campbell and John A. Williamson.
Ibid., 78.

Orienting Inquiry:

---

1.   Now that I have been assigned a student teacher, what must I do to prepare?

2.   How do I make a good beginning impression of a competent teacher?

3.   How should I orient the student teacher to my style, my students, and the school?

"He has half the deed done, who has made a beginning."
              Horace   Everyman

The most stressful period of a pre-teacher's professional background is reached at the very onset of the student teaching experience. In most cases student teachers are placed with cooperating teachers with little attempt to match teaching philosophies, styles, personal interests, and individual personality traits. A student teacher naturally is apprehensive about the pending relationship. "Getting along" is crucial to professional success and the choice of an ideal pairing is usually out of the hands of the student teachers. In fact, the second highest area of stress experienced by the student teacher is his concern about the relationship with his supervisor. (1)

The cooperating teacher can reduce much of this apprehension and tension early in the experience. Acquaint yourself with the background and interests of your student teacher and find out about his educational background, work experiences, personal characteristics, hobbies, and professional ambitions. Most colleges/universities ask the student teacher to supply this background data at the time of his application to student teaching. If you do not receive these data from the institution, you should request such information directly. You may want to use a request data sheet for the student teacher to complete prior to your first meeting with him. The following guide may help you to decide the kind of information that would be useful.

Student teacher data sheet for the cooperating teacher

1. Name, home state/country
2. Areas where you have lived and traveled
3. Previous work experience
4. Prior labs or classroom experiences
5. Career goals
6. Hobbies, interests, special talents
7. Honors
8. Favored subjects, topics and areas; least favored subjects and areas of study
9. Major concerns or anxieties about entering the student teaching experience
10. A list of topics or tasks that you would like to attempt during your assignment.

Meet with your student teacher prior to "that first day in the classroom." A fifteen minute talk in a mutually comfortable environment helps to alleviate anxieties of the introduction. If possible follow up by inviting the student teacher for a school lunch (but necessarily duty-free) or meet at his college lunchroom or snack area. Wherever or whenever, limit the agenda to an informal get together and avoid all procedural necessities and routines at these early encounters.

Many cooperating teachers experience stress or apprehension during the student teaching experience for a variety of concerns which may include:

Will our personalities or teaching styles clash? Will the student teacher be more popular with the students? Will I be too dominant or too easy going? Will I lose the student discipline that I've worked so hard to establish? Can I evaluate fairly? Is it possible to guarantee the time necessary to observe, give feedback, and plan with the student teacher? How can I be the best possible role model? Can I assure the principal that the curriculum will move along on schedule?

These are genuine and typical concerns of cooperating teachers. The solutions usually are discovered as the two of you work in a "team approach," addressing openly all anxieties during the experience.

The Initial Conference

Once you know the student teacher informally and have some background from his data sheet, you must institute procedures necessary for the most productive initial professional conference. The manner, organization, and relationship established in this meeting sets the pattern for all subsequent conferences.

First provide essential information concerning the community, school, curriculum, and background on your student population and their parents. Compile a handbook which includes rules, reminders, calendars, objectives, philosophies, and projects. A sample guide is included in the appendix section. This handbook should be given to the student teacher at the first conference. Assign the handbook for reading homework along with a request for questions about procedures or content.

In the initial conference limit the information giving to essentials. Save a major portion of time to discuss the worries, apprehensions, and concerns of your student teacher. Make it a time for sharing ideas, feelings, and attitudes. Indicate that worry sessions may be a frequent and essential component of the total experience. Vow that no worry will be allowed to build up or get out of hand.

Also allow some time for sharing textbooks and materials, but let the student teacher know that you expect a written list of questions about the materials and handbook. This list of his questions will help to form the agenda of the next meeting.

Before concluding the conference, ask your student teacher to begin to compile a long range series of major goals that he would like to achieve during his experience. Have him include in his list the learning objectives for content, intellectual skills, and processes expected of the students. This assignment, when completed, should produce an overall framework of professional objectives, goals, and major teaching trends. This task will help him with his overall philosophy and should benefit him in his new job as a student teacher.

This initial conference is the first step toward forming a stable, productive, open, and joint-evaluative relationship. It will set the stage that you take your responsibility as a teacher in a serious manner and will encourage him to do the same.

In one of the early conferences with your student teacher, you should explain the preferred and acceptable dress code, as well as unacceptable behaviors. Today, few dress code rules exist, but the student teacher may benefit from your experiences as a professional teacher and your knowledge of a particular administrative preference. Occasionally a beginner may choose to dress or behave in a very casual manner which could take him out of the teacher model role and put him in competition with the students. Explain to him that there may be selected days to be casual such as field trips for science, rallies, or even designated "jeans and sweatshirt days."

Student teachers also should be informed as early as possible of school rules and procedures that are written or expected school policy. For example, if the faculty is expected to report at 7:45 and leave at 4:00 the student teacher should know this on his first day of observing, not after a week of drifting in at 8:15. Explain other school rules such as chewing gum, eating, drinking, or smoking at inappropriate times or places. Confrontations can be avoided through open communication and by supplying a logical or philosophical reason for supporting the enforcement of regulations. Include a list of school policy for absences, vacations, snow days, etc. in the handbook you give to him.

In preparation for your initial meetings you may appreciate hearing some wishes or stated concerns of former student teachers:

"I hope that we will get along and if not as close friends, at least as respected professionals."
"I hope that my cooperating teacher will provide information about the students so I can know what to expect and perhaps understand the reasons for misbehaviors and attention-seeking students."
"Can I get access to resource materials and use the school's audiovisual equipment?"
"Will my cooperating teacher introduce me to faculty, administrators, guidance counselors, and staff?"
"I wonder if she will include me in extracurricular activities so I can feel like a real teacher?"
"How soon will I be teaching all subjects to all students?"

Although there are many different qualities and expectations listed for the "ideal cooperating teacher," the general overtones are very similar. You must be supportive, open, and informative. As you plan for the student teaching experience, it will be helpful to remember these needs, concerns, and desires stated by previous student teachers as they were about to meet their cooperating teachers for the first time.

Preparing Your Classes for the Student Teacher

Your students will want to know what they can expect with a student teacher helping them. Establish a mood of excitement and anticipation. You should provide students with some interesting information about the student teacher. Depth of explanations will vary according to the grade level and the general awareness of your students. However, all students should be informed that they will be a very important element in helping the new teacher to get to know the school and the students. Each student should be encouraged to learn the student teacher's name, watch for the chance to help him to find things or places, and to make him feel welcome and at home in this class.

In some cases, especially in an elementary setting, you may encourage your students to prepare a welcome note to the student teacher with some of their own creative ideas. You could mail these notes to him prior to the first day of his visitation. This type of activity eases some of the apprehension of the student teacher. It also allows him to surprise students by knowing some of their names and recognizing some of their writing skills or talents, even on the first day. Some student teachers keep this communication going by writing periodically, even after the experience is over.

You also might have several students prepare a welcome sign or bulletin board for the arrival of the student teacher. Students can help with organizing a place in the room for the student teacher to work. Other students might be assigned to show the student teacher around the school. The more positively involved your students can be in preparing for the student teacher, the smoother the transition will be.

The First Day

The formal introduction of the student teacher to your class can set a positive influence on the entire experience. The introduction must be professional but enthusiastic. The student teacher should be given the same status as a teaching peer, using the formal "Mr., Mrs., Miss, Ms." title with the last name. Once the student teacher has been introduced, it is helpful to relate some interesting background information or an anecdote which enhances his prestige to the students. Encourage the candidate to say a few words, react to the welcome, or even question the students about things he notices or would like to have answered, in an attempt to get to know the class. Also request that the students give their names and tell something significant about themselves or to ask a question that they would like the student teacher to answer. Encourage the student teacher to take several minutes with this activity. Suggest that he may want to jot down ideas or student names during the introductory session.

Assign the student teacher a desk or work area that is reserved for his use alone. This gives him a feeling of ownership and shows the students that they can go to this person at this place in the room for a private conference or for help with work.

The student teacher should be included into the teaching/learning experience on his very first day. For example, he should be given the role book and asked to make his own seating chart. This activity promotes an early learning and use of students' names. He also should be encouraged to move around the room to answer individual student's questions. Assign him to work with small groups and to help prepare materials. Let him know that you would like him to list observed teaching strategies or behaviors that seem to yield specific results. These observations will be discussed at later conferences on "strategies." Early involvements ease tension and remove the status of "outsider." They also prepare the student teacher to maximize the learnings available to him during his experience by teaching him to be a good observer.

Encourage your student teacher to attend planning periods and lunch with you so that you can get to know each other better. It will also allow you the opportunity to introduce him to other faculty members, traveling teachers, secretaries, and school staff. If you have other specific school duties during that first day, include your student teacher in these responsibilities, sharing "survival" pointers that you utilize for effective management.

Be professional at all times. Do not criticize or evaluate other teachers or administrators nor label particular students as trouble makers. Refrain from all prejudicial or biased statements which may give the student teacher a misleading first impression of both your professional demeanor and the school's students or staff.

During the first day, it is important for you to hold your first mini conference. Encourage the student teacher to ask questions and express concerns about the experience up to this point. React to these questions and observations. Ask him to list in a formal notebook all future questions either for self-analysis or for discussion in subsequent conferences. Let him know that both of you will learn best by analyzing the kinds of questions asked, and the self analysis and answers attempted by the student teacher. The questioning component and mini conferences are all part of the program to help him to develop into an informed, self-educating, self-sufficient, and confident teacher.

At the end of the first day hold your first formal two-way conference. Solicit questions and concerns that the student teacher may have accumulated from the first full day. Offer feedback and reinforcement for commendable teacher-related behaviors that you have noticed throughout the day. Do not hesitate to mention behaviors or strategies you feel may eventually be non-productive. (not "good or bad" but "productive or nonproductive"). Review or complete the assignments from the handbook and seating chart. Begin to set up some guidelines so that future long and short range planning activities can begin. It is recommended that you produce a timeline calendar, indicating increasing responsibility for teaching activities by the student teacher. He could begin with short selected activities for particular classes and then proceed to a full time unit for one class. Add other class responsibilities gradually until he assumes the "full load." Save some time in your overall plan at the end of the session to ease off assignments to allow time for school wide observation and involvement.

Conclude this first day on a positive note and give much emphasis on your feelings that he will be a success in your classroom. Suggest to him that if he has any problems to discuss that he may call you at home. Most student teachers do not abuse this privilege and it is comforting for them that you appear to be a professional and a friend "after school hours." You know how important the school day after 4:00 is to your success in teaching. Some help during this early experience in "after school" management will be greatly appreciated by a student teacher.

PROBLEM ANALYSIS No. 13: A BAD FIRST IMPRESSION

In the initial meeting with your student teacher you feel that he acts blase' and almost "laid back" or perhaps even uninterested in the upcoming experience. You ask for "concerns" but he says that he isn't worried because "nearly everyone can teach fourth graders." You ask him to look over the handbook that was prepared for him, but he responds "I went to this school as a kid. The rules never change." There are many items and helpful suggestions in the handbook and you are sure that he will need to know many of the inclusions. Other attempts to introduce the clinical model approach or the request for his long range goals are brushed off as "unnecessary or busy work." You are not pleased with his lack of enthusiasm or his attitude in general.

MAKING DECISIONS:

Would you demand that he read the handbook and produce a report on its content and a list of goals and specific dates? Can you ignore this negative attitude? How do you prepare for the next meeting?

PROBLEM ANALYSIS No. 14:   SENIOR BOYS EMBARRASS
                            GRACE

Grace, your new student teacher, is very
attractive. She is bright and full of enthusiasm
and wants to make English fun for your high
school students. When you introduce her for the
first time to one of the required remedial
English sections, several senior boys whistle and
make suggestive comments. They then ask her if
"she teaches as 'good' as she looks." You are
somewhat annoyed with their behavior, but Grace
is shocked, embarassed, and does not know how to
react. She can't respond and looks desperately
to you for help.

MAKING DECISIONS:

What is your response to the boys' actions?
Do you encourage Grace to say anything to the
class or wait until a later time? What is your
approach to Grace when you have the next
conference with her?

PROBLEM ANALYSIS No. 15:   OVER-ENTHUSIASM
                            CREATES A WORRY

In your early planning conference you map
out a calendar for easing Brenda into a full load
of teaching by gradually adding one class at a
time. Full responsibility may occur near the end
of the third week of student teaching. She is
quiet while you present your rationale, but when

60

you ask for her reaction, Brenda states that for many student teachers this may be a feasible plan. However, she feels that she has a great deal of experience and would like to begin full time teaching in two or three days. You are surprised by this request.

MAKING DECISIONS:

What are the arguments for and against granting this request? Does Brenda need to become acquainted with the students, procedures, or even you as a role model? What plan would you follow to achieve the best of what both of you want out of the session?

PROBLEM ANALYSIS No. 16:   IS THIS THE TIME TO BEND THE RULES?

When you explain the basic school rules and policy to David, he looks disturbed and says that he cannot arrive by 7:45 each morning because of "personal conflicts." He tells you that he can arrive by 8:15 or 8:20, always before classes start. You know that this barely allows him to walk into the room before the first bell and that he will not be there for early preparation or to perform preschool duties and responsibilities.

MAKING DECISIONS:

Do you ask David to explain the "personal conflicts?" What are the implications if you drop this rule? What reasons would you give if you insist that he must act as a professional and abide by the same rules as the rest of the staff?

1. As a major project (one which teachers can use with future student teachers) assign each person in class to compile a student teaching handbook for his particular school, grade level, and unique situation. The information provided in the appendix includes a framework of topics which could be incorporated. Encourage creativity and utility as well as flexibility for change in the construction of this manual.

2. Role play in class several possible introductory meetings between cooperating teacher and student teacher:

a) nervous student teacher and empathetic, conscientious cooperating teacher.

b) know-it-all student teacher and surprised cooperating teacher.

c) self-confident, enthusiastic, and personable student teacher and laissez-faire cooperating teacher.

d) underachieving student teacher and organized, zealous cooperating teacher.

Have the observers in the class evaluate the effectiveness of the cooperating teacher in each role and offer suggestions for alternative procedures.

3. Discuss apprehensions that your students may have in working with student teachers. Which of these could be discussed openly with student teachers that might be of benefit to both parties?

NOTES: CHAPTER 4

1) J.E. Morris and G.W. Morris. "Stress in Student Teaching," _Action_ _in_ _Teacher_ _Education._ 2:4 Fall, 1980, 57-62.

Orienting Inquiry:

---

1. How much help will the student teacher need to plan successfully for content, procedures, and means of evaluation?

2. What is the best procedure for promoting adequate daily and weekly plans?

3. As a cooperating teacher how do you justify the need for detailed planning?

4. Do team teaching activities interfere with the student teacher's independence in planning?

> "At the very heart of teaching
> is the bridge of trust between
> teacher and student and this
> bridge cannot survive rigidity
> and hiddenness on the part
> of the teacher." (1)

The on-going process of planning between you and the student teacher is a bridge to successful teaching. Your approach to this joint effort serves to promote interest, awareness, openness, and self-confidence for the student teacher. It will show him that you feel that planning is critical for organization and subsequent student learning.

In an early meeting before the actual pencil and paper work, it is important for you to probe for concerns that the student teacher feels may affect the success of the experience. Surprising and unexpected anxieties may surface. For example, the following comments have been reported by new student teachers:

"What will I do if the students do not like me?"
"I am nervous about being observed and evaluated."
"Will you want a lesson plan for each lesson?"
"How long in advance must I prepare required lesson plans?"
"How do I decide just what to teach?"
"I may not know enough subject matter and I may make mistakes harmful to students."
"I may not have enough free time for planning, grading papers, and preparing materials."
"What if our teaching styles conflict?"
"I have seen how much enthusiasm you have during the whole day. I don't think that I can keep it up."
"What do you expect me to wear?"
"I am really afraid of losing control of the students because I don't think that I can keep order and discipline with your system."
"I don't think that I can be creative without causing chaos."

The emphasis and direction of the subsequent discussion will vary with each student teacher. Listen carefully to your student teacher before you supply help, a quick reaction, or even casual reassurances. Let him know that all concerns can be attacked through a joint effort. Explain to him that you will provide suggestions if he would like the advice. The moments spent in a discussion such as this will show the student teacher that you are eager and willing to help. Early efforts like these make the planning sessions less traumatic and will encourage the student teacher to exert the extra effort to do his best to impress a "real professional."

"WHAT DO YOU START ON FIRST?"

Rationale for Planning

Sometimes student teachers do not understand why so much time needs to be spent in the planning process. Do results warrant the effort exerted? We recommend that in an early meeting with your student teacher you discuss some of the advantages of conscientious planning, perhaps citing personal examples from your own background. The following list includes ten supportive statements for planning which you may want to highlight.

1.   Teachers plan to familiarize themselves with the content of the lesson. Planning often takes the form of study so that the teacher feels comfortable with the subject matter. Confidence gained through this type of study helps lessen the concerns about potential student questions.

2.   Planning is necessary in order to accumulate the appropriate materials or learning aids for the right day and time. It is not always possible to obtain necessary equipment or special instructional supplements within a day's notice. Advanced planning can help to assure that you will have the desired curricular materials when needed.

3.   Teachers need to plan activities that are appropriate for the constraints of the school's physical setup as well as for consideration of other classroom teachers. You would not be too popular if you decided to spend several noisy class periods using dramatics or role playing if nearby classrooms were having tests. Advanced planning with other teachers eliminates confrontational problems.

4.   Planning is essential if you are attempting to meet individual student needs and differences. As a student teacher learns how long it takes for students to complete various tasks, his planning will begin to incorporate activities for students of varying abilities.

5.   Planning is a confidence-building technique. A well-developed lesson plan should provide one with security to know where he is going with a concept. An inexperienced student teacher who tries to "fake it" usually falls flat because he is shaky with his objectives and procedures.

6.   An organized plan can be a preventive measure against classroom chaos and disaster. Students sense teacher disorganization and are quick to join in on the unstructured lesson-in most undesirable ways!

7.   Planning allows a teacher to prioritize teaching objectives. If one has a sense of the

importance of goals for students he can begin to make judgments about essential versus trivial learner outcomes. If time or outside interruptions become a problem it is easy to reject the less important goals and not panic over lost time and valuable lessons.

8. Teachers who plan carefully and organize their lesson plans in a sequential order are more likely to vary their methods of presentation. An organized planner can examine procedures to see if a pattern of too many lectures and not enough inquiry activities exists.

9. If a teacher allows adequate time to plan ahead he is more apt to include other variables such as learner interests, community needs, and creative suggestions or ideas into his overall goals, rather than using a textbook approach.

10. The teaching/learning process cycle is more effective with better planning. A lesson plan can be used later as a guide in analyzing and evaluating strengths and weaknesses. This exercise in critiquing will help to improve future plans.

Types of Planning to Require from a Student Teacher

Comprehensive planning includes designing both long and short range plans. A long range plan is a unit plan of a series of experiences related to a specific topic and developed in a meaningful combination and sequence. Involving the student teacher in this planning process provides a solid basis for cooperation. Long range planning efforts foster communication and provide the student teacher with a road map for comprehensive planning and recognized expectation. (2)

Student teachers often are caught up in the whirlwind of daily planning, grading papers, handling discipline problems, and preparing materials to the extent that they neglect the total picture--the long range plans. Therefore the cooperating teacher must work with the student teacher to produce major overall goals. The student teacher can fit the daily activities into the overall unit plan.

Most education majors are required to develop a unit of instruction for pre-student teaching classes. However, the unit planning process becomes reality when the student teacher must implement objectives, prepare activities, and secure a means for evaluation. Encourage the student teacher to develop several units of instruction for each subject area. Help him to reduce dependence upon the use of the textbook for every lesson. Explain that each unit can vary in length, but the time needed for each plan must be established carefully. Each unit should have stated multi-disciplinary relationship themes and should allow for interaction by children with exceptional abilities. The following sample guide for a unit may be useful.

Each unit of instruction should include:

-Purpose-why is the unit being taught?

-Learning objectives-what will the students be able to do upon completion? (Objectives will include content, process, and attitude development skills)

-Activities-include materials, directions, and evaluation plans.

-Means for evaluating the total unit (content, process, and attitude changes should be measured)

-Outline of plan for teaching (how you plan to structure your time) ex: day 1: activities 4,7 (25 min.)

-Resources for children (books, films, filmstrips, records, resource persons, teacher-made activities, etc.)

-Resources and background information for the teacher.

Helping the student teacher to develop daily and weekly instruction is known as short range planning. Assist the student teacher to develop daily instructional objectives and to select appropriate and available materials. Help him to facilitate instruction by suggesting teaching methods and strategies for each short range plan. Show him how to use the results of student tests to indicate needed instruction or additional activities.

Daily lesson plans should be thorough, precise, and detailed during the early weeks of student teaching. Begin to limit your input as you encourage the student teacher to assume more of the initiative.

The following sample daily lesson plan will serve as an overview and example of what a cooperating teacher should expect to be prepared by the student teacher for each class to be taught. This suggested plan or one which you develop should be included in the student teacher handbook.

I. Purpose/Objectives

What do you hope to accomplish in this lesson? What student behaviors (concepts, processes, and attitudes) do you expect? What skills should the students demonstrate?

II. Materials

What materials will you use throughout the instruction? (You should include such materials as books, films, computer or a.v. equipment, maps, charts, teacher-prepared or student-prepared aids, games, etc.)

III. Procedures

Development--How will you begin and present the lesson? (Include your interest-provoking first question.)

Creativity and motivation--How will you maintain student interest throughout the lesson?

Closure--How will you draw conclusions for the lesson?

IV. Evaluation

How will you evaluate concept/content mastery, process and skill attainment, and attitudes developed? How will you ascertain the effectiveness of your teaching? How will you measure appropriate activities for exceptional students? How will you evaluate the multidisciplinary applications and inter-relationships attained?

You should require the daily lesson plans at least 24 hours prior to instruction so that necessary modifications can be made. Under almost no circumstances should a student teacher be allowed to teach a full lesson without any written plan. This practice is unfair to you and to the students.

Many administrators at various levels re-quire that teachers submit weekly lesson plans in advance for their perusal and approval. It will help a student teacher to establish direction and clearer goals if you encourage him to meet this same requirement. The weekly plan need not be in full detail like the daily plan. A sample first week's plan is presented for your examination. You may choose to work out such a plan with your student teacher early so that his responsibilities are established clearly.

Goals for the Student Teacher-Week One

Monday:
Learn students' names as reasonable. (Secondary teachers will have more names to attempt.) Observe cooperating teacher. Note various teaching techniques. Help with extra duties. Work with individual students and small groups. Be prepared for a conference with questions and comments about the first day.

Tuesday:
Examine curriculum guides and texts. Observe. Notice students who answer and those who don't. Continue with extra duties, small group help, etc. Co-teach an activity class. Plan for a short lesson for Thursday.

Wednesday:
Observe. Watch and take notes on disciplinary techniques. Consider your own strategies and develop a system to implement. Read article to class. Continue with duties and help for students. Participate in conference to discuss lesson plan. Submit a second lesson plan for an activity for Friday.

Thursday:
Present lesson in the subject area discussed at Wednesday's conference. Observe difference of student reactions, if any, to your teaching. Continue with expected duties. Discuss the strengths and weaknesses of the first lesson.

Friday:
Teach lesson. Write a self-evaluation of the first week. List goals for yourself. Continue observation and duties. Help with grading papers for the week. Begin to plan a bulletin board which you will put up Monday.

Potential Problems with Conflicts in Lesson Planning Methodology

Cooperating teachers and college supervisors may differ in philosophy and practice for writing lesson plans. If there is a severe clash, the student teacher may be squeezed in the middle in a very uncomfortable position. Possible disagreements can arise over the type of objectives needed, for example specific behavioral objectives or more general goals. Other issues may involve length and detail to be expected in daily plans or the type of evaluation to be written and followed. For example, some college supervisors prefer a two-part evaluation, one for students and one for a self-critique following the lesson. Other conflicts may involve the deadlines for submitting plans prior to teaching.

In our experience a three way conference is the most successful method to resolve differences. This technique allows expectations to be understood and agreed to by all three parties involved. Generally it is advisable for the student teacher to be thorough and follow the tougher set of requirements (within reason) during the student teaching experience. The cooperating teacher and college supervisor can agree to loosen up if the student teacher is spending too much time on the planning process and not enough time for other duties.

Planning Cooperative Instruction

Encourage opportunities to team teach with your student teacher. This technique requires cooperative planning so that both parties can introduce ideas, background knowledge, provide available resources, and exhibit special talents. This type of teaching is commendable and enriching for both elementary and secondary classrooms. The successful interplay and joint effort are appreciated by students of all ages.

Team teaching is therefore a way of combining the planning and instructional efforts of two or more teachers to utilize individual abilities in some advantageous way. Team teaching also provides a system whereby new and inexperienced teachers can observe teaching methodologies by experienced colleagues and receive immediate and informal feedback about their own teaching performance. (3)

When planning cooperatively, both teachers determine their respective roles and responsibilities during both instruction and evaluation. This technique of team planning and teaching can be used to strengthen the instruction at special times, but it should not be used for the entire student teaching experience.

SHARING IDEAS - PLANNING

M	T	W	T	F
REMINDER: 3 WEEKS TO QTR. GRADES !!! HEARING TESTS GIFT/TALENTED SCREENS	**1** ASSIGNMENTS !! CURRENT EVENTS - LOCAL NEWS TESTING - WEATHER &, WEATHER PREDICTIONS HAND IN PROJECT REPORTS POST & REVIEW ALL POSTERS - FOR LAST UNIT	**2** BEGIN NEW SCIENCE UNIT ON SEEDS. FILM "CAREERS IN BIOLOGY" (PERMISSION SLIPS -PREPARE DITTO MASTERS	**3** FIELD TRIP TO AG SCHOOL LABORATORY - GREENHOUSE 2 HOURS - BUS DISCUSSION: "GERMINATION"	**4** PREP: SOAK SEEDS FOR GERMINATION ANATOMY OF SEED LAB 2-3 MUSIC PROGRAM AUDITIONS (LAST PERIOD MUST MAKE UP LAB)	**5**
7 "SEEDS" LAB CON'T. -EQUIPMENT!! PLANT WATER ETC.	**8** CURRENT EVENTS: STATE NEWS LAB LIBRARY RESEARCH TIME RESERVED: Mrs. Zompkins -"SCIENCE CAREERS"-	**9** SCHOOL YARD- SCI FIELD TRIP COLLECTING WILD SEEDS - PREVIEW VIDEO TAPE FOR PURCHASE -	**10** LAB ON SEEDS - SORT · CLASIFY · SET UP FOR GERMINATION HEARING TEST 9-12pm (MAKE UP SHEETS)	**11** MEASUREMENTS OF SEEDLINGS DRAWINGS DUE WATER PLANTS SCI IEP's DUE FOR SPEC. ED. CONFERENCE : ST. TEACHER 4PM	**12**
14 IEP's PLANNING CONFERENCE 8am FILM STRIP - "PLANT GROWTH" - DISCUSSION SHEET -	**15** CURRENT EVENTS - NATIONAL NEWS FRUIT & SEED PRODUCTION LAB - (FRESH FRUITS) REMINDER: NAT'L. GEOGRAPHIC TV 8:30 "WORLD BIOMES	**16** REVIEW & DISCUSSION OF PLANTS UNIT PRE-TEST SHEETS	**17** TEST ON PLANTS SCIENCE FAIR: ANNOUNCEMENTS SHOW " PROJECTS" SLIDES ASSIGN - "DESIGNS"	**18** DESCRIBE & DISCUSS / DESIGNS FOR SCIENCE FAIR PROJECTS COLLECT SCI NOTEBOOKS FOR GRADING	**19**
21	**22**	**23**	**24**	**25**	**26**

Decide on which topics would lend themselves to such team effort early in the planning sessions so that both cooperating teacher and student teacher can search out resources for their part of the organization. Team teaching offers an excellent learning experience for both persons and strengthens the professional relationship. "Team arrangements can enhance the feelings of participation and control congruent with the idea of self as a professional educator." (4)

Flexibility in Planning

Student teachers need to learn that if it is Friday at 10:30 they may not be discussing page 32, problem 7 as indicated in the lesson plan. You will need to reinforce the idea that a lesson plan is a guide for instruction and no more. Assure them that they can abandon their lesson plans in many instances. The following examples might be cited to them:

-Students may be confused, not learning by the intended method of instruction.
-Disciplinary problems are interfering with learning.
-Student interest or curiosity lends itself toward a different, yet worthwhile direction.
-Special resources (student brings in a guest from Iceland, etc.) are unexpected and available on a limited time basis.
-Current events (special successes or tragedies) are more significant to the development of your students than your intended issues.
-School interruptions may create time conflicts.

Reinforce the need to be adapatable in his planning. He may not need to throw out a lesson completely. He may need to change objectives or procedures to adjust to student needs and interests. Encourage your student teacher to be courageous and creative. Flexibility is one of the characteristics of an A+ teacher!

76

In conclusion, the necessary efforts that you direct toward planning will be an indication of your success with your student teacher. Major efforts must be extended to make the objectives of education, the major themes of instruction, and the overall purposes of curricula evident, relative, and important to the daily activities of the classroom.

PROBLEM ANALYSIS No. 17:" --NEVER WRITTEN A LESSON PLAN?"

Bob turned in his first lesson plan and you are suspicious of his ability to develop an adequate written plan. You suggest that he rewrite the plan and include the several missing portions. Bob tells you that he never learned how to write a lesson plan. You find that situation hard to believe because you have had well-prepared student teachers from the same institution with the same instructors.

MAKING DECISIONS:

Do you teach Bob how to write an adequate lesson plan, ask him to work back through his college department, or do it all on his own?

PROBLEM ANALYSIS No. 18: A ONE MAN TEAM?

In an attempt to team teach a unit with George, you suggest that the two of you develop a unit on basic geometry concepts. When you present this idea at a planning session, he remarks that he would prefer that you do the unit alone and choose the sequel unit for him to plan and teach. He does not give a reason for this desire to avoid the team teaching approach and you have no clues as to why he appears to want no part of it.

MAKING DECISIONS:

Should you probe until you know the reasons for George's rejection of the teaming concept? Should you back off and try again on a much later unit? Or should you insist that there is no choice and this is the proper time and place to fulfill one of his requirements.

PROBLEM ANALYSIS No. 19:   A DEFENSE FOR LONG
                           RANGE PLANNING?

You recommend that Ellen design a two week unit plan for poetry. She responds in a suprising way. "I have seen your long range plans and frankly you have never been on schedule because of all the interruptions and your tendency to take off in all directions. It is a waste of time and effort to produce the long range plan. I'd rather try to take one day at a time so that I know what I'm doing."

MAKING DECISIONS:

Should you comment on her attack? Should you defend yourself and explain the variations in flexible planning and implementations? Should you encourage the procedure of only using short daily plans? Should you insist on the long range plan because it is a requirement from the college and/or because you see the need?

PROBLEM ANALYSIS No. 20:   GREAT LESSON PLANS--
GREAT TEACHING: UNFORTUNATELY THERE IS NO
CONNECTION

Phyllis has been with you for three weeks.
She can write meticulous and detailed lesson
plans and includes all the necessary components.
When she teaches, however, you can see little
connection or resemblance to the written lesson
plan. She teaches well and the students respond
eagerly. This success and achievement come as a
complete surprise to you because you have no idea
what to expect. Objectives are being met but so
far not those objectives that have appeared in
the lesson plan.

MAKING DECISIONS:

Is this a major problem? How would you
help Phyllis to recognize and deal with this
discrepency? How can you correct the problem and
yet preserve the fine work that she is doing?
Should you let Phyllis proceed without
intervention?

PROBLEM ANALYSIS No. 21:   WHO MAKES THE RULES?

At an early planning session with Katrina
you ask for a thorough lesson plan for her first
teaching assignment. She informs you that "with
her college supervisor's support, she will use an
abbreviated daily block form plan for her lessons
because she is always well-organized." You do
not feel comfortable with this response.

MAKING DECISIONS:

Should you speak with the college supervisor to verify Katrina's position and ability? Do you demand a lesson plan with specific requirements? Would you allow Katrina to use this simplified format and hope that she sees the benefits of the more thorough lesson plan?

Applying Ideas:

1. Group students in pairs to role play one as a student teacher and one as a cooperating teacher. Assign them to prepare a team lesson of their choice along with an adequate lesson plan. Copy lesson plans and share these efforts with entire class.

2. In small groups discuss and determine an appropriate length of time that the student teacher should have to prepare and present both short and long range plans before they are submitted to the cooperating teacher for study. How long should the time period be between the cooperating teacher's inspection of the plans and the student teacher's implementation into the classroom activity?

NOTES: CHAPTER 5

1)   Jo Ann Taylor.   "A   College Supervisor Speaks
to   Student Teachers,"   Kappa   Delta   Pi   Record.
v.20 n. 1 (Fall, 1983), p. 20.

2)   L. David Weller.   "Essential Competencies for
Effective   Supervision   of   the Student Teacher,"
Education.   104:   213-218,   Winter, 1983.

3)   Johanna   Kasin   Lemlech.   Curriculum   and
Instructional   Materials   for   the   Elementary
School.   New   York: Macmillan   Publishing   Co.,
1984, p. 377.

4)   James   A. Beane and Richard P. Lipka.   Self-
Concept, Self-Esteem and the Curriculum.   Boston:
Allyn and Bacon, Inc., 1984, p. 68.

Orienting Inquiry:

---

1. How keen is an "effective observer?" What does he notice about the teaching/learning process?

2. Are there systems or techniques for collecting accurate and measurable data during observations?

3. Are there ways to observe and collect data without threatening the student teacher?

"Genius, in truth, means little more than the faculty of perceiving in an unhabitual way."
William James from <u>Psychology</u>

Top-notch cooperating teachers know how to be good observers. Their observation skills include much more than an occasional glance while grading papers to check if the student teacher is in control of the class. Researchers, however, criticize the cooperating teachers' performance as observers. Zimpher, de Voss and Nott (1980) also report that most cooperating teachers are not interested in observing student teachers. They also state that most cooperating teachers attempt to involve the student teacher in teaching the full curriculum within one week of placement. (1)

It is the initial observation process that gives the cooperating teacher baseline data needed for all subsequent comparisons. Carefully documented notes taken while observing are vital to successful conferencing and discussions of achievement. The data collected are essential for periodic evaluation of progress. The more effective and accurate you become at recording observations, the more help you can offer the student teacher.

To help the student teacher be at ease while being observed, you should encourage him to keep observations of your teaching while you still have responsibility for the class. Because of your experience and knowledge of the environment, this task and the following discussion shouldn't be threatening. In fact, this experience should serve as a model for your student teacher. Reward the student teacher's ability to take accurate notes, recognize strategies, and in general evaluate or question you as the role model. Suggest some of the following points to observe and promote.

Student Teacher Checklist for Observing the Cooperating Teacher			
Often	Seldom	Not obsv.	
			Does the teacher: acknowledge students equally and fairly?
			move around the classroom and share time with each group?
			adjust voice and tone for emphasis and clarity?
			appear organized and ready for the sequence of activities?
			give simple and easy to follow directions?
			vary teaching strategies during the lesson?
			ask appropriate questions for feedback and review?
			ask intellectually challenging questions to promote thinking?
			use a variety of positive reinforcement strategies?
			try to promote positive attitudes from all students?
			develop respect for learning? handle disruptions calmly?

Encourage the student teacher to share his thoughts with you after each observation period. Most will hesitate to mention negative feelings or challenge your motives for fear of alienating your friendship. With your support and encouragement these observations and honest questions will give the new teacher better ideas about the art of successful and efficient teaching.

OBSERVING THE COOPERATING TEACHER

"WHY DOES SHE DO WHAT SHE DOES?"

After several days of observation the student teacher should recognize consistent strategies that you use to maintain discipline, promote time management for seat work, and stimulate discussion sessions, group work, and activity-related situations. When he feels comfortable with his own success in observing and learning from your teaching, he then can begin to teach several lessons of his own.

Your amount of actual time needed to observe and record data for the student teaching experience will differ with several of the following variables:

-initial student teacher competence in teaching skills
-his experience with classroom management techniques
-guidelines established by your school administrator or the college program
-perceived feelings and /or attitudes of the students and their parents
-amount of self-confidence expressed by the student teacher
-amount of confidence you feel in the abilities of the student teacher.

As in any general guidelines, an important courtesy to recognize is moderation. It can be disturbing to the person being observed if he never feels the independence and confidence necessary to survive in the teaching profession. On the other hand, a casual, laissez-faire approach (total independence and a "sink or swim" attitude) can be catastrophic as well. Therefore it is suggested that the number and length of the observation periods be reduced as the student teacher gains success and confidence. Subsequent observations can be unobtrusive, spontaneous, and can vary in length and frequency. They will enable you to maintain an evaluation of the teaching pattern without suffocating the student teacher.

"WHICH DIRECTION FOR EFFECTIVE TEACHING?"

What Does An Effective Teacher Look Like?

Researchers studying teaching have begun to answer some important questions concerning the effectiveness of teachers as judged by direct observation of teaching and of student achievement. A recent study has included in its findings a list of eight factors that constitute an effective teacher. An interesting point is that through their analysis of 127 assessment scales or opinions of effective teaching only four of the eight desired behaviors were found on half of the scales. We would like to share the eight most effective teacher characteristics in a prioritized listing for your consideration during observation sessions.

Effective Teaching Techniques

--Clarity and organization
--On-task behavior of students (time
   management and effective discipline)
--Use of feedback to students for improving
   performance
--Task-oriented climate
--Warm, supportive environment
--Flexible, adaptive teaching
--Enthusiastic teacher
--High expectations of students' abilities
                                        (2)

Observations of student teachers should be on-going and multiple and relate directly to student attitudes and learning. The remainder of this chapter is designed to help you become a more effective observer by providing a variety of techniques to collect data.

Techniques for Improving Observation Skills

The seven techniques described below allow you to select the most appropriate methods for collection of the right kind of data necessary for productive conferences.

Technique 1: Use of Informal and Written Remarks

Early in the observation experience before specific behaviors are targeted for observation, the cooperating teacher may choose to use a very informal approach of jotting down general comments, suggestions, class behaviors, and unusual events. This process is a subjective technique because of its generality, but can be a useful one if shared in a conference session with the student teacher.

After discussion of the written remarks it is advisable to give the student teacher this list of suggestions and comments to study. These informal notes and subsequent mini conferences serve to remove ambiguity and uncertainties and increase the appropriate direction needed to follow.

This technique unfortunately is the only method that some cooperating teachers ever use throughout the entire supervisory period. It is essential that you add other suggested observation techniques so that adequate and specific data pertaining to teaching behaviors and instructional strategies can be collected in an objective format.

Technique 2: Collecting Data on Student Behavior Using a Seating Chart Approach

This technique is used to note which and how many students may be on or off task while someone else is conducting the lesson. This is a fairly easy technique to implement. Construct ditto master copies of a seating chart with ample squares for each child's name. Code only two or three behaviors for which you would like to collect data. Make three actions the limit so that your notes are not cluttered with excessive details. Decide upon how frequently you will record the behavior during a set time period. (Note: every 3-5 minutes should provide ample data.) The following example may provide a model. The eight students are observed every 5 minutes for a period of 30 minutes, totalling six observations per student.

Visual Record of Student Behavior for 30 Minutes

Sally	Paul	Julie	Joe
1-1-1	1-2-1	2-3-1	2-2-1
1-1-1	1-2-2	1-3-3	1-3-1
Aaron	Chad	Mark	Joan
3-3-3	3-2-1	2-2-2	1-1-1
2-1-3	1-1-2	1-1-3	3-1-1

Key to behaviors for this observation:

1) On task and conscientious
2) Disruptive behavior such as talking, playing, or out of seat
3) Quiet and not disturbing, but off task (doing something other than work assigned)

Each block (designated student for observation) will have six numbers, each recorded at five minute intervals from the key which you set up. The eight students whom you have chosen to observe in this manner are then ready to analyze for the recorded behavior. It is difficult to observe an entire class in this manner, so you may choose to select a sample of 5 or 10 students to monitor.

Observing and recording different behaviors each time will enable the student teacher to examine a number of potential problem areas. The student teacher may request specific observation of some skills he is trying to perfect. Encourage the student teacher to apply this same technique during a lesson that you plan to teach. Comparisons and discussions will be beneficial and can facilitate planning and improvement of instruction.

Technique 3: Observing and Recording Student Teacher's Performance on a Checklist of Teacher Effectiveness

During an early conference between the cooperating teacher and student teacher, it is necessary to design a checklist of teaching behaviors that both feel are important attributes of teaching effectiveness. Be sure to consider the research mentioned earlier in the chapter when designing an appropriate checklist. This list or part of the list can then be used for observation. Each area can be examined and evaluated if written comments are added to each category. The structure and organization of the checklist help focus in on individual teaching techniques and behaviors and assure the student teacher that you will be observing specific techniques. It is advisable to emphasize quality examination and evaluation of several pinpointed areas rather than to attempt to use the total checklist for every observation. A sample observation sheet used by a liberal arts college education program is provided to illustrate the ease with which this technique can be fulfilled.

Observation Checklist

Subject_____   Date_____
Time_____   Group Size   _____

	EX.	G.	SAT.	U.	N.A.
Teaching Behaviors and Characteristics					
Attitude and behavior					
Voice quality					
Knowledge of subject					
Movement around the room					
Preparation					
Organization					
Flexibility					
Meets indiv. needs					
Interdisciplinary re-lationships					
Lesson					
Appropriate level					
Use of hands-on experiences					
Use of audiovisual aids					
Appropriate timing					
Student Behaviors					
Respect shown					
Motivated					
Student interaction					
High interest level					
Enjoy challenges					

Technique 4: Observing Verbal Interaction in a Classroom

The ability to measure and evaluate verbal interaction in a classroom is another valuable technique. Assessment of interactions can help the student teacher to identify and analyze differences in students, recognize teacher actions versus student actions, determine the percent of teacher talk, and to identify the intellectual level and verbal interaction that occurs in the class.

Flanders' Interaction Analysis system is used by many supervisors to collect useful verbal data for conferences. The Flanders' system can yield the data required to identify and classify verbal interaction. If there is a tendency for your student teacher to dominate or monopolize interaction in the classroom, use the Flanders' grid to gather data on the amount of teacher verbal time versus student time. Interpreting the data may help the student teacher reassess strategies or questioning techniques and help him to see the need to involve students more actively in the teaching/learning process.

The Flanders' Analysis System requires you to recognize ten classes of verbal interactions (see chart). The observer records data on the chart every three seconds. At the conclusion of the observation period an analysis of the teacher's and students' verbal behavior can be deduced. Distinct and informative comparisons can be made between response comments (categories 1,2,3) which indicate an indirect style of teaching and initiation remarks (categories 5,6,7) which reflect a direct style of teaching. Flanders does not categorize the "asking questions" (category 4) as either direct or indirect.

It is recommended that if you choose to use this system that a longer period between observations (10 to 30 seconds) will allow more time to record comments and allow for a greater diversity of teacher activity.

SUMMARY OF FLANDERS' INTERACTION
ANALYSIS CATEGORIES

Teacher Response	1.	Accepts feelings or attitudes of students in a nonthreatening way.
	2.	Praises or encourages students to answer.
	3.	Accepts or uses ideas of students. Builds on student ideas.
Talk	4.	Asks questions to students.
Initia- tion	5.	Lectures, citing facts and opinions.
	6.	Gives directions or orders.
	7.	Criticizes student or justifies authority.
Student Talk	8.	Student responds to a teacher contact. Limited freedom of expression.
	9.	Student expresses his own ideas. Freedom to develop opinions.
Silence	10.	Silence or confusion. Unclear to observer.

Based on Ned A. Flanders' <u>Analyzing Teaching Behavior,</u> 1970.

Justification for the use of Flanders' for analyzing student teacher verbal interaction is supported by Dunkin and Biddle. They explain Flanders' "law of two-thirds" which describes the dominance of teacher talk. Two thirds of the time spent in classrooms is comprised of talking; two thirds of this time is occupied by the teacher; and two thirds of the teacher talk consists of giving directions, expressing his own ideas, and criticizing students.(3) Student teachers need to be aware of the ease in which teachers can dominate classroom discussions. Moderations of the Flanders' System can be valuable for both the student teacher and the cooperating teacher to gain a greater insight into the total teaching effectiveness of both persons.

Technique 5: Analysis of Questioning Strategies

Perhaps the one strategy that has the greatest effect on class interaction and the level of intellectual challenges is the ability to ask the right kinds of questions at the appropriate time. This strategy must also be accompanied with procedures which help to get the most out of each question asked.

As a background for using this technique, you must be able to distinguish among types of questions asked by a teacher and to sort all questions into one of two categories: convergent and divergent. Convergent questions require single correct answers. (What is the capital of Hawaii?) Divergent questions encourage critical thinking, use of past experiences, weighing and considering, seeing and understanding potential relationships, associating, and promoting individual creativity. Divergent questions can be answered in several alternative logical ways. For example, an answer to the following question would promote several thinking skills. (How might you account for population increases in Hawaii over the past twenty years?)

It is also necessary to be able to identify and recognize the level of cognition required by the students to take part in answering each question. One system widely used is the Taxonomy of Cognitive Domain (Bloom). You must be able to assess each question to determine which level of mental activity is required to produce an answer.

UTILIZING BLOOM'S TAXONOMY FOR QUESTIONING SKILLS

Intellectual Level	Description	Example
Knowledge	emphasizes recall and re-cognition of facts.	What are the names of the planets?
Comprehen-sion	student must translate in-formation to demonstrate understanding.	What is the meaning of this para-graph?
Appli-cation	student must use previous information in a new way.	Classify the musical instru-ments by the way they sound.
Analysis	Student must draw conclusions, determine evidence.	Give examples to show if the author is using fantasy or reality.
Synthesis	use large pieces of data in a creative way.	Design a germ-free environ-ment for use on the moon.
Evaluation	students make a judgment on a set of condi-tions.	In your opin-ion do you feel the playwright was sensitive to prejudice?

For the most effective teaching, questions from each level should be used at some point in every lesson. It is distressing, therefore, to find that the great majority of questions asked by classroom teachers seldom require more than recall, comprehension, and application. Teacher made tests generally focus on these three lowest levels as well.

During the classroom observation jot down a short version of each teacher question asked. List examples of the kinds of questions given and then classify the question into the appropriate Bloom's category. The following questions and notes from a fourth grade social studies class serve as an example.

-How is the Japanese environment different from our American environment? (Analysis)
-What is the capital of Japan? (Knowledge)
-Describe the occupations of people living in Tokyo. (Comprehension)
-Name the major export industries. (Knowledge)
-What are your ideas about the most distinct features of Japanese culture? Put your ideas into a creative mode. (Synthesis)
-Why do you think that the Japanese scientists , their discoveries in computers, radios, cars, and other high technological industries are doing so well in comparison to other countries? (Evaluation)

In a summary of the major questions asked, the student teacher should be complimented if he included questions from all cognitive levels. Conduct sample observation sessions which focus on questioning techniques. Encourage the student teacher to work toward providing higher level questions for each lesson plan. Suggest that the student teacher key each question asked for several lesson plans.

Technique 6: Observing Movement Patterns

Another observation technique involves recording the movements of the student teacher and/or students during a lesson. Acheson and

98

Gall (4) describe movement as an important process to observe because patterns can indicate confidence levels, affect the classroom discipline, and indicate teacher bias in the area of the room that receives most teacher attention. It is suggested that you use a ditto sheet of the seating chart with tables, desks, and doors indicated for a basic worksheet.

Draw continuous lines and arrows which indicate teacher movement. Use X's for stopping points. You may want to devise a timing system to indicate the relative periods of attention between movements. A sample movement chart is provided for your consideration.

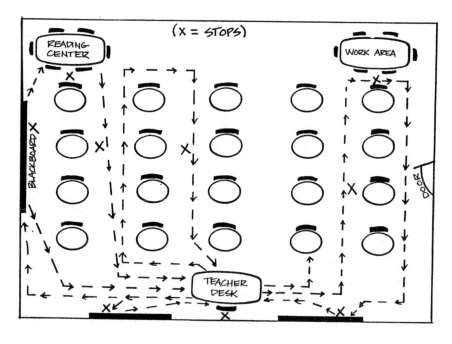

VISUAL RECORD OF MOVEMENT

Encourage the student teacher to analyze his own movements, and to note any trends and patterns which emerge. It will be helpful to observe several times during the experience so that different patterns may be discovered.

The data supplied may help to change procedures. Awareness and knowledge of student and teacher behavior may have an impact. For example, you may notice that the student teacher tends to remain near the front desk and blackboard to the extent that discipline, attention, and interest fall off for the students in the rear of the room. Excessive motion during a lecture or instructional activity may increase student frustration and promote disinterest. Therefore, use of modified versions of movement patterns as a tool may help to produce an aware and more competent student teacher.

Technique 7: Using Video Tapes and Sound Tape Recordings

Another useful observation technique utilizes the capacity of permanent records made by an audio and/or video recorder. These "observers" allow the student teacher to see and hear exactly how the class lesson progressed. If a video recorder is not easily accessible, a tape recorder can be used with much success. It is advantageous to record short segments of several lessons (10-15 minutes) and try to record many different types of instructional techniques. Again, encourage the student teacher to evaluate each strategy and suggest alternative procedures which may be more effective. Most portable tape recorders will pick up much of the instructional procedure and many of the student comments. Unfortunately (or perhaps not!) excessive classroom noise renders the tape hard to interpret, to check voice levels and tones, and to listen to grammar and context. Send the tape recording of a short lesson home with the student teacher for a self-evaluation of two or three items that you think should be analyzed. This observational technique is one that will help the student teacher to see the teaching as it is, not just as you perceive it.

Deciding Upon Techniques

You will not have the time to utilize every observational technique suggested nor will you choose to use each technique as presented by the authors. However, all of the techniques suggested are easy to use for any given grade level or subject area. To be a successful and useful observer, you must be able to collect accurate data, interpret results, and record and produce concrete, systematic, and effective methods for sharing observations with the student teacher. As more data are collected and shared during frequent conferences, the chance for self-confidence in the student teacher will increase. Your interest in his career will be obvious because the goals and objectives of successful and effective teaching will be the major emphasis of each conference.

PROBLEM ANALYSIS No. 22: "MY COOPERATING TEACHER
                        DIDN'T QUITE MEASURE UP"

You have asked your new student teacher to observe, analyze, and critique your approach to discipline. Later, during your conference, you ask for her reactions to your methods. She looks somewhat reluctant to answer, but then says, "My college instructors taught me not to punish or embarass a child verbally in front of the class, which you did when Jason, Lisa, and Tod misbehaved. They said that you should reward students who measure up to your expectations. I have never seen such well-behaved students, but they were never praised by you. Are theory and practice really this different?"

MAKING DECISIONS:

How do you respond to this judgment of your teaching? Are theory and practice different?

PROBLEM ANALYSIS No. 23: MISDIRECTED OBSERVATION

Lisa, your new student teacher, has been observing the teaching/learning process for several days. You notice that she is busy writing during your teaching. When you ask for her written observation data, she admits that she was writing letters. She had no comments regarding the class, student behavior, or the teaching strategies you were utilizing. In general she said that everything was just fine and she didn't have any questions.

MAKING DECISIONS:

Should you remind Lisa that her behavior is not quite professional? How and when should you spell out your dissatisfaction? Do you need to list the requirements of an observation and conference session?

PROBLEM ANALYSIS No. 24:   AN UNWELCOME
                           SUGGESTION

As Sandra completes her first week of student teaching you mention to her that she appears to be extremely soft-spoken and you fear that many students will be unable to hear her. You suggest that you would like to use a tape recorder so that she can judge her volume and perhaps learn to adjust it accordingly. She politely tells you that she would not like nor appreciate you or anyone else taping her lessons. You are surprised by her polite, but insistent refusal.

MAKING DECISIONS:

Should you be assertive and insist that she hear her own teaching on tape? What would be the implications of stepping back and respecting her refusal? What action would you take?

PROBLEM ANALYSIS No. 25: "MY COOPERATING TEACHER'S OBSERVING IS THREATENING"

During a formal observation using specific pre-discussed techniques, you notice that Sara is nervous and appears to be upset. She loses her continuity and goes blank. She notices you writing notes and she begins to cry in front of the students.

MAKING DECISIONS:

What should you do? Do you step in and finish the lesson? leave the room? take her out of the room and talk with her? How would you handle the problem?

1. Assign each class member one class period to observe. Have him utilize two observation techniques to assess your teaching. At the conclusion of each class, have the student to report his observational findings, interpret data, and discuss results. Your students may find this activity uneasy at first, but they will realize that they will have to play the same role if a student teacher is encouraged to observe them. Other students should be asked to make additional comments or suggest alternatives.

2. As a homework assignment ask students to develop a potential observation or data collecting technique that they could use with student teachers that is not included in this chapter.

3. Which technique might be the most beneficial to the student teacher who wants to improve his overall teaching effectiveness to reach more students? Discuss in class.

NOTES: CHAPTER 6

1)   N. L. Zimpher and G.G. de Voss and D. L. Nott.   "A Closer Look at University Student Teacher   Supervision," Journal   of   Teacher Education.   31 (4), 11-15.   1980.

2)   Helen E. Fant,   Carl Hill, Amelia M. Lee, and Rosalyn Landes.   "Evaluating Student Teachers: The National Scene," Teacher Educator, v. 21 n. 2, p. 2-S, Autumn, 1985.

3)   M.J. Dunkin and B.J.   Biddle.   The Study of Teaching.   N.Y.:   Holt,   Rinehart,   and   Winston, 1974.

4)   Keith Acheson and Meredith Gall.   Techniques in the Clinical Supervision of Teachers- Preservice and   Inservice Applications.   N.Y.: Longman, 1980. (119-125).

Orienting Inquiry:

1. How do you decide if you need to have a conference?

2. What role does the cooperating teacher play during the conferences?

3. What is the purpose of three way conferences?

4. How do you handle the "uncomfortable conference?"

5. How do student teachers perceive the value of time spent in conference sessions?

> The word, even the most contradictory word, preserves contact--it is silence which isolates.
>
> Thomas Mann (The Magic Mountain)

It is easy, if the student teacher is progressing , to limit or reduce the number of conference sessions. There is, however, a definite need for regularly scheduled formal and informal conferences during the entire student teaching experience for all categories of learners.

A formal conference should be held weekly at an agreed upon time to discuss current curricular plans and strategies, to analyze the data from observation sessions, and to evaluate the student teacher's progress.

Informal conferences should be frequent and spontaneous to assure open communication. These conferences may be only five or ten minutes in length and may vary widely in topics. For example, discussions may cover immediate discipline problems, administrative functions, suggested teaching strategies, or perhaps recognition and support for a job well done.

The authors especially support the statements by David Weller in his discussion of the value of time used for spontaneous conferences. "Conferences conducted in an informal setting encourage student teachers to ask questions, raise concerns, and be candid about expressing their opinions. With this kind of frequent communication, the supervising teacher provides continuous support and encouragement while challenging the intern to become more creative and independent in task performance." (1)

It is an important role for the cooperating teacher to assure that both formal and informal conferences occur throughout the experience. The student teacher must be aware that communication is encouraged and helpful.

Establishing an Environment for Productive Conferencing

Many researchers have found that the cooperating teacher usually dominates the interactions during conferences. Barnes found that as much as 72 percent of the input came from the cooperating teacher while only 18 percent came from the student teacher. The two most frequently discussed topics at the conferences involved conversation of specific classroom events and procedures or suggestions given directly to the student teacher. (2) Usually student teachers simply acknowledged what the cooperating teacher had said. Over 24 percent of all student teacher comments were of this acknowledgement type ("o.k., yes, fine, etc.) (3)

Certainly you, as a facilitator of student teachers, want to provide meaningful direction for them. However, you must allow adequate time for listening and for topics that go beyond the immediate or the important. The best method to approach a conference is to search out general concerns and comments from the student teacher.

Listen carefully and respond to these statements and questions. Then, if the concerns are given adequate attention, present (without evaluative remarks) the types of data which you collected during an observation. It may, for example, include a ten minute tape, a chart of student behaviors (objective in nature), and a checklist of teaching performance (more subjective). Ask the student teacher to analyze each source of data. His evaluative statements will serve to point out areas or procedures that were not as effective as they might be. Ask the student teacher, "If given the chance, how would you do the lesson differently?" Limit your own comments to positive feedback and reinforcement of praiseworthy efforts unless the student teacher finds no faults with anything. If he finds no need to change nor any reason to modify any procedures, you may need to supply the overlooked or neglected aspects of lesson.

The student teacher then may ask for your specific reactions and you should respond in an honest way. This is the appropriate time during the conference for your contributions. Add comments, suggestions, and guidance needed to plan for future changes. Assess his self-analysis and supply evaluative statements which you have prepared prior to the conference session. Share these observations with the student teacher, but delete those statements that he has already noted in his self-analysis. O'Neal discovered that many cooperating teachers prepared evaluative remarks in journals and other written assessments, but did not share these judgments with the student teacher during any conferences. (4) If one does not receive adequate feedback throughout the experience, he does not know what he must do to be effective and successful.

Encourage your student teacher to keep a notebook which lists in chronological order the lesson plans, self-evaluations, observational data, your evaluations, and the products or suggestions from each conference. It is much easier to make comparisons, see self-improvement, and recognize the areas which still need attention. This effort to organize his results

109

will allow both of you an opportunity to measure more accurately the progress that has occurred.

Major Topic Focus During Conference Sessions

In an analysis of supervisory conferences, over two-thirds of the discussions concentrate on the cognitive domain. Griffin also notes that the emphasis on conversation is placed on cognitve issues and concerns. These issues can include topics such as lesson plans, evaluation strategies, teaching skills, observation techniques, or preparation of audio-visual aids and other materials. These cognitve areas involve any plans concerning thinking skills for teacher, student teacher, and/or learner. Griffin also notes that little attention is given to the affective dimensions of school and classroom life. These areas can include personal and interpersonal aspects of schooling such as cooperation, valuing, appreciating, etc. Areas which received the most attention during the supervisory conferences, instead, were those of materials and methods. (5)

The cognitive planning sessions are relevant and needed. However it is important for you to insure that a portion of each conference is used to consider planning for affective growth in students. Include discussions of appropriate and effective student grouping and sizes, student needs and interests, background information which may help to clarify student behaviors, and values that you would like to instill in your students. The following list of suggested topics may help to guide conference planning. Some topics may be covered only once, while others may appear in nearly all conferences.

110

NOTE: A CONFERENCE IS A CONFERENCE, IS A CONFERENCE, IS A CONFERENCE, IS A CONFERENCE...

AS LONG AS IT IS "OPEN", "FAIR", & "BASED ON TRUST & UNDERSTANDING".

ALL OTHER MEETINGS FALL SHORT!

SUGGESTED TOPICS FOR CONFERENCES: A CHECKLIST

Management and Information Topics

Information regarding school, faculty, community
Rules, regulations, philosophies
Time schedules and changes
Resource suggestions
Extracurricular activities
Seating charts, needed materials

Cognitive topics (Intellectual skills, content directive,   teaching strategies)

Expectations
Observation techniques
Sample lesson and unit plan
Characteristics of an effective teacher
Evaluation strategies (content and process)
Teaching methodology

Affective Topics (Feelings, worries, attitudes, perceptions, etc.)

Personal insights concerning students
Personal problems of either student or cooper-
  ating teacher
Values to stress; motivational strategies
Student needs, interests, problems

Three Way Conferences

It is desirable that you and your student teacher arrange for three or four way conferences. Many principals and school administrators may be interested in an active role in the training process for student teachers in their schools. They may share in supervising the student teacher, including observations and conferences throughout the semester. Many college programs require a written evaluation of the student teacher from the building administrator. This requirement influences the amount of involvement by the principal.

The college supervisor may participate in or coordinate several three or four way communications during the experience. Most student teachers recognize that active participation by the college supervisor adds strength to the learning experience. In fact, a researcher reports that contrary to what some of the literature suggests, the university supervisor is perceived by student teachers as playing a vital role in their professional development. These students stated that the university supervisor is effective in three major areas: developing attitudes, handling of the observation process, and the manner in which feedback was given. (6) The college supervisor also supplies useful information about the college program, answers questions regarding requirements, attempts to resolve conflicts, explains assignments, defines procedures, and assists with the grading process.

If a team conference seems threatening to your student teacher or to you, keep in mind that it serves to keep you informed of progress and lessens the secrecy and mystery of a single event evaluation procedure. All parties can express and discuss expectations, raise questions, share concerns, clarify ambiguities, and compare data and evaluations.

The responsibility of assigning a letter grade or its equivalent can be a shared role when you have open three way conferences. If this final evaluation includes the work of the student teacher, a review of the semester's products and results, your efforts at supervision, and the gains shown by the students, it becomes a professionally enriching experience for all parties. It allows for a more valid documentation of evaluation as well.

The Uncomfortable Conference

Every student teacher is different in experience, ability, and personality, so the chance for total happiness and comfort in every conference session is slim indeed. If you are honest and "up front" with the student teacher, you will need to criticize, to clarify necessary procedures, and perhaps lay down the law to preserve professional judgments about teaching, learning, and students.

Reactions to your remarks and attitudes will vary. Some student teachers will agree with you totally and welcome suggestions for change. Others may be defensive, feel insulted, or even resentful. Some individuals may express feelings only by non-verbal mannerisms (facial expressions, changes in voice, different sitting positions, etc.) while others may be quite vocal in response. If you have taken enough time to collect data and present it fairly and encourage mutual evaluation, your suggestions may upset, but not devastate the student teacher.

The best way to handle what you suspect may be one of those " uncomfortable conferences" is to allow the student teacher to self-critique his lesson first by examining data. Allow him to render his own interpretations. Keep the focus on positive aspects and constructive re-planning. Let past errors, when once obvious and discussed, die a quick death. Help the student teacher to plan more effectively so that corrections are noticeable and success is more attainable. With consistent guidance and time for reflection or a chance to implement changes, the student teacher will see the value of confrontation, especially honest self-evaluation, as an aid toward becoming a mature and competent professional. Remind him that sometimes you are unhappy with the evaluations of your principal, but that everyone in the education process is concerned with the same goal of maximal learning and the development of self-concept in students. All conferences should be geared toward these goals.

Importance of Effective Conferences

Free and open communication between cooperating teacher and student teacher is essential. Researchers have indicated that student teachers spend 80 percent of the professional communication time with their cooperating teachers. The remainder of the professional verbal contacts were divided among university supervisors, other teachers in the building, and other student teachers. The cooperating teacher must ensure that conferences are frequent, helpful, positive, and important to the student teacher.

It is interesting to note that the need for communication and direct support appears to decrease over the experience. Student teacher questions and topics required about 42 percent of the conference time during the first week, but declined to only 8 percent by the seventh week. (7) Your input, therefore, changes accordingly over the same period. Your availability and initiation are most important for productive conferences during the early weeks of student teaching. As the experience proceeds, you may choose to have fewer informal conferences, but maintain the weekly formal conversation. Although student teachers may have fewer questions, they continue to need your support and evaluation of their progress. The importance of effective conferencing techniques can be best summarized in the following quotation by D. Weller:

"By adopting the Carl Rogers concept of "caring" the supervising teacher provides a foundation upon which free and open discussions of attitudes and values can take place, building a positive relationship based on fairness, praise, and constructive criticism. Building a climate around honest communication, based on mutual trust and empathetic understanding, the supervising teacher fosters an environment which supports effective teaching and learning strategies." (8)

PROBLEM ANALYSIS No. 26: "NO THREE WAY
CONFERENCES!"

Hank is having problems with student teaching that you feel are serious enough to warrant a three way conference which includes the college supervisor. When you mention this idea, Hank asks that you keep the conferences private and if necessary notify the college supervisor. It is not clear why he feels this way about a three way conference.

MAKING DECISIONS:

Have you collected enough data to take any action? Should you honor Hank's request and try to work things out between the two of you? Should you call the college supervisor and discuss the problems privately? What other alternatives may be just as beneficial?

PROBLEM ANALYSIS No. 27: HELPING TO MAKE
PROFESSIONAL DECISIONS

Your student teacher is a perfectionist and is overly critical of her own teaching progress. After several weeks of teaching, she asks for a conference with you to evaluate her work. You have several sources of data which indicate that she is doing quite well. For each observation there are a few suggestions for improvements or alternative procedures. You in no way feel that

116

the observations are negative.

You therefore are quite surprised when she tells you that she knows that she will never be good enough to make it in education. She says that she would like to quit and drop out of student teaching at this time.

MAKING DECISIONS:

Could any student teacher examine the data and be this disappointed with her level of success? Do you think she is just looking for more praise and wants you to talk her out of her decision? Should you involve other people (administrators, counselors, college supervisor, etc.) in this dilemma?

PROBLEM ANALYSIS No. 28: ASSERTIVE AND OVERBEARING AUDREY

Audrey has an assertive and somewhat overbearing demeanor. She appears to have all the answers (often before a question is asked). At conference time you offer your best advice to help her to improve and to remove weaknesses in her teaching. She defends her methods and is not willing to change or try different techniques. In a specific instance you insist that she attempt a different approach, and she agrees verbally. After several days, however, there is no evidence that Audrey is going to follow through.

MAKING DECISIONS:

Do you give up on the new methods or insist on an immediate demonstration of her attempts? How could you work out a better conferencing system to achieve goals you feel are not being addressed?

PROBLEM ANALYSIS No. 29:   TOO QUIET FOR COMFORT

Heather, a very shy student teacher, is hesitant to ask questions or offer comments during conference sessions. She acknowledges your remarks in a positive manner, but you cannot tell how she feels about her experience. Your attempts to elicit response or reaction meet with "I'm not sure," or "it's o.k. with me" or "I just don't know."

MAKING DECISIONS:

How can you help Heather to take a greater responsibility in assertive self-evaluation and self-interpretation roles you feel are fundamental to the teaching/learning enterprise?

PROBLEM ANALYSIS No. 30:   "I ONLY NEED A 'C' GRADE"

Joe is fulfilling requirements of student teaching to receive a degree in physical education. His efforts are minimal, his enthusiasm poor, and his interest in the classroom students lacking. At the third conference you explain that you do not believe that he is working up to his potential. He responds with the remark, "I only need a C from this experience, so I only need to work that hard. I do not want to become a teacher. I just want to get this experience behind me."

MAKING DECISIONS:

Should you accept the lack of effort he expends on your students? What is the best way to proceed with this problem? How do you handle your methods of evaluation? Is this attitude fair to your students?

---

1. In pairs, outline an agenda for six potential student-teacher cooperating teacher conferences. Include agenda and materials required for the conference.
   a. planning for a semester schedule
   b. designing a field trip
   c. arranging for a guest panel for discussion
   d. preparing for an open house
   e. getting ready for a parent conference
   f. establishing a three way conference with the college supervisor or principal.

2. Discuss the strengths and weaknesses and the value of time spent in conferences.

1) David L. Weller. "Essential Competencies for Effective Supervision of the Student Teacher," <u>Education</u> 104: 213-218. Winter, 1983.

2) Susan Barnes. "Student Teachers' Planning and Decision Making Related to Pupil Evaluation." Texas University, Austin: Research and Development Center for Teacher Education, Feb., 1983.

3) Sharon F. O'Neal. "Developing Effective Planning and Decision Making Skills: Are We Training Teachers or Technicians?" Tex. Univ.: Austin, Tex.: Research and Development Center for Teacher Education, March, 1983.

4) Sharon F. O'Neal. <u>Ibid.</u>

5) Gary A. Griffin. "Student Teaching and the Commonplaces of Schooling." Texas Univ., Austin: Research and Development Center for Teacher Education. April, 1983.

6) Lynn C. Smith and Donna E. Alvermann. "Field-Experience Reading Interns Profile the Effective/Ineffective University Supervisor." Paper presented at the Annual Meeting of College Reading Association. Atlanta, GA., 1983.

7) William Johnson, C. Benjamin Cox, and George Wood. "Communication Patterns and Topics of Single and Paired Student Teachers." <u>Action in Teacher Education.</u> v.4 n.1 p. 56-60. Spring/Summer 1982.

8) David Weller. <u>Ibid.,</u> 1983.

Orienting Inquiry:

1. How do you rationalize teaching effort and competence into a grade or its equivalent?

2. How effective are cooperating teachers in their evaluations of student teachers?

3. What guidance is available to help assess student teachers' progress? Are there models to follow?

4. Other than a "letter grade" what else should the final evaluation indicate?

> "Today there is pressure from students, teachers, school boards, and state legislators to create real and meaningful learning situations that are evaluated in real and meaningful ways."(1)

The evaluation of a student teacher is a necessary but sometimes unpleasant responsibility of the cooperating teacher. There is no single test or checklist that translates performance into measured results or evaluated success. "There should be an abundance of literature on how supervisors rate students, on whether they can rate reliability, and on what criteria they seem to emphasize. Unfortunately---and surprisingly---there is a paucity of studies relating to these questions." (2)

Lack of easy evaluation solutions is only one concern in assessing competence in our student teachers. There is also heavy public pressure for the improvement of teachers. Opinion polls continue to reflect dissatisfaction of teachers' abilities to handle their numerous responsibilities. "While no sector of the educational enterprise has escaped unscathed, much of the rhetoric has focused on the unsatisfactory performance of America's teachers. Curiously, the proposed solutions are themselves symptomatic of a condition often discussed in the supervision literature: a lack of attention to problems associated with the marginal teacher." (3) These pressures are most deeply felt by cooperating teachers who must decide on the competency levels of student teachers. They must weigh and consider the interests and efforts of the student teacher against the potential thousands of learners with whom he may have the opportunity to influence during a teaching career.

To achieve the most reliable assessment, a cooperating teacher must conduct a thorough on-going process of evaluation. The ultimate goal should not be limited to the final report or grade, but should be a major part of the student teacher's educational development. Throughout this evalution, the student teacher should be encouraged to diagnose his own strengths and weaknesses and help to plan for potential remedial activities to correct deficiencies. Final grades should therefore reflect the student's ability to be self-aware, self-evaluative, and self-correcting. A final analysis should not be a surprise to anyone who is involved in the on-going evaluative process.

The effective evaluator will help to develop appropriate goals, organize materials, and develop a plan with the student teacher that outlines the essential ingredients and abilities to be measured. He will also outline the data to be collected and the methods of assessing total procedure. The student teacher should be encouraged to take an active role in this planning/assessment process so that no hidden evaluation tactics occur throughout the experience.

Planning for Evaluation

Effective evaluation requires several different methods of assessment and necessitates observation and analysis of a variety of examples of teaching behavior. During early conferences it is important to discuss the roles and values that the evaluation process can serve in changing teaching approaches.

An early consideration during this planning session is the overall philosophy of the evaluation experience. You will want to incorporate views of your student teacher and yourself as well as those specified by the college or university education department. Most institutions require a type of summation assessment, usually in the form of a letter grade or a pass/fail statement. A research study of various institutions in seven midwestern states includes data that 46% of education departments utilize the traditional letter scale, 43% use pass/fail, and 11% use alternative methods. (4) The cooperating teacher and student teacher must discuss the college's expectations for evaluation to determine the kinds of data that need to be collected for yielding clear results. Different systems of grading may influence a student teacher's attitude for commitment. Therefore as a cooperating teacher you will need to have a thorough and specific evaluation system in place so that your student teacher will be encouraged to exert maximal effort. These are important discussions to have in these early planning stages.

Another topic that should be included in the evaluation planning session is the cooperating teacher's list of clear expectations required of the student teacher. A frequent complaint from the student teacher is that "I thought that I had completed everything, but at the end of the term I found that my efforts were not in line with the cooperating teacher's expectations. I can't believe I was given a B!"

One researcher found that student teachers failed to receive adequate specificity from cooperating teachers regarding expectations. The requirements from supervising teachers were often global and generalized. He concluded that it is likely that "if expectations for an experience are lacking in clarity and precision it is possible that the experience itself will be lacking in clarity and precision." (5) Without clear expectations, the cooperating teacher makes evaluation much more difficult and possibly unfair or unjust.

EVALUATION: "IS IT MY BEST PROFESSIONAL JUDGMENT?"

Clear communication is one of the major
success tactics for the evaluation planning
session. If on-going evaluation procedures
indicate continuous negative results or
weaknesses, the total evaluation picture will be
affected. This situation is magnified if you are
not communicating, if one speaks while the other
does not listen, or if communications are hidden
by innuendo or casual comment. A cooperating
teacher must be willing to share evaluation
strategies and collected data with the student
teacher at frequent intervals. You must state
openly and often in writing the conditions which
must be met, procedures that must be allowed, or
assignments that should be completed or redone.
The discovery of early problems should be flagged
for attention so that steady growth and
improvement are possible. Surprises are not
welcome at the final evaluation session.

Are Cooperating Teachers Effective Evaluators?

Researchers of supervision have been rather
critical of the ability of cooperating teachers
to grade student teacher competence with
precision and adequacy. In a review of over
25,000 student teacher final letter grades,
researchers reported that 70% (nearly 20,000)
were given an A's in student teaching. Another
18% received B's, 2% received C's, .25% earned
D's, and .08% (or 21 students) received F's.
Their conclusion was that "the prevalence of high
grades makes one wonder what an A or B in student
teaching really means." (6) Perhaps the general
grade inflation in all fields of education during
the 1970's explains some of the high marks.
Other legal factors may have influenced the ease
of providing A's. It was also reported by
another researcher that student teachers,
cooperating teachers, and university supervisors
all tend to rate one another's performance
highly. (7) In research of a major university
teacher education program, it was reported that
the cooperating teachers appeared to grade almost
all of the student teachers highly and that they
are even more inclined to overestimate or make

errors on the side of leniency when they are familiar with those whom they are rating. (8) Another evaluation study of secondary student teachers is indicative that high student teacher ratings do not necessarily mean that a high level of pupil cognitive achievement occurred during that experience. (9) It appears that the grades given to student teachers reflect finishing the experience with little or no connection with the recognized excellence or listed deficiency traits that occur during the time. The authors feel that practicing professionals who accept student teachers generally are capable evaluators who for a variety of reasons tend to grade generously by some other set of criteria.

These reports create an uneasiness in the public's view and promote the search for the source of blame for many of the problems in education. It is not surprising, therefore, that cooperating teachers face their role of evaluating student teachers with apprehension and dislike. The student teacher has legal access to the cooperating teacher's remarks, and can use college or university records, stated negative comments, or written evaluations. Supervisors, in this threatened position, may feel that they have to evaluate more leniently or supply only positive or supportive data in the records. Whatever the reasons may be for inflated grading standards, cooperating teachers and university supervisors must try to use care and discretion in their evaluations and provide evidence for a particular grade.

There are many cooperating teachers who accept the responsibility of evaluation with great planning and success. Research was conducted on both elementary and secondary cooperating teachers in terms of their effectiveness in evaluation. Researchers found that cooperating teachers reliably rate student teachers in terms of two major factors: preparation and presentation. The major difference between the elementary and secondary cooperating teachers' evaluation emphases were that the elementary teachers placed the major importance on the student teacher's ability to organize, analyze, and synthesize student

128

responses, while the secondary supervisors placed primary emphasis on the communication skills. In all cases of student teacher evaluation, they found that classroom skills were more important than competence in content. (10) It is evident from this study that cooperating teachers <u>can</u> evaluate in the areas of preparation <u>and</u> presentation, most likely because these areas can be defined with expectations and measured in observable ways.

The answer to accurate and comprehensive evaluation includes careful planning, effective observation, accurate documentation, and frequent communication. It is obviously a responsibility of the cooperating teacher to help a student teacher to perform at a level of proficiency consistent with at least a minimum professional competency. The cooperating teacher, therefore, has an influential responsibility to determine the adequacy of the student teacher to enter the teaching profession. Final grades should reflect these judgments. No other single recommendation or evaluation is as critical as your assessment of competency to both the success of the teacher education student and to the students he may or may not influence in reaching his potentials.

Types of Evaluation Models and Strategies

The following three models are presented in a brief format so that cooperating teachers and administrators may select portions of any of the systems that they may feel successful in using. There are some overlapping concepts in the models as well as merits and weaknesses. The cooperating teacher or administrator may choose to use a combination of ideas.

1. Horizontal Evaluation Model

The horizontal evaluation model is a type of intra-individual developmental approach to assessment of student teachers. Gitlin defines horizontal evaluation as a system based on the premise that the aim of evaluation should be the personal and professional growth of the student teacher. This evaluation procedure does not compare the student teacher to other individuals nor does it rank individuals by skill competencies. The aim of horizontal evaluation is to expand the scope of evaluation so that the theory learned by the student teacher is linked to practice in the classroom. An important aspect of the model is one designed to help student teachers to expand and question the goals that guide their practice.

Gitlin recommends three types of evaluation within the horizontal framework. One area of growth involves the student teacher's ability to develop several clearly stated teaching intents, representing a broad scope of educational issues, based on an understanding of what is possible. This skill will require the student teacher to analyze the types and needs of students in the class and adapt appropriate teaching strategies to meet these needs. A second criterion that Gitlin recommends for evaluating student teachers in a horizontal method is to assess their ability to actualize their intents into practice. After an appropriate analysis of proper methods to use, can the student teacher implement them sucessfully? The third criterion for horizontal evaluation of student teachers is their ability to be self-critical. More specifically, by the end of a student teaching experience, the student teacher should be aware of incongruity between intents and practice and should be able to suggest alternatives (either in his intents or practice) to make the situation more congruent. This self-awareness and self-critiquing is a high level of analysis and evaluation which should be attained for a successful career in teaching. (11) The need for the horizontal evaluation model might be supported in the study by Wheeler and Knoop. They presented findings that student teacher evaluations are significantly higher than either college or cooperating teacher evaluations. (12) This finding may imply that more work is needed in areas of self-assessment and self-critiquing during the student teaching experience.

The benefits of a system such as horizontal evaluation have been examined by other researchers who have determined that because of the self-analysis demands of the model, that the same framework used in student teaching can also apply to the examination of one's teaching long into the future. (13)

2. Vertical Evaluation Model

The vertical evaluation model used in student teaching is a skill-based and individual achievement based model. In this type of model the emphasis is placed on accountability, the assessment of a student teacher's mastery of a set of competencies. It also can be referred to as a competency-based model. The philosophy behind this approach is that to evaluate student teachers the cooperating teachers must first identify the skills or competencies essential to good teaching. Evaluators using this model therefore observe teacher behavior to determine if competency has been achieved. Defino explains that the larger the performance data base, the stronger the conclusions one may draw about the student teacher's work. In addition, performance statements may be organized according to extant formal evaluation criteria. Therefore, supervisors are likely to obtain pertinent information for summative evaluations. (15)

If a cooperating teacher chooses to use a competency-based evaluation model, the following breakdown may be helpful. A teacher may utilize three categories for closer evaluation: knowledge of subject matter, teaching performance, and teaching products (lesson plans, case studies, learning materials, etc.) (16) Each of these categories can be assessed both individually and collectively to provide a better overall assessment of a student teacher's specific strengths and weaknesses.

The advantages of using a vertical or competency-based model of evaluation are provided by Smith and Stevens (1984). They state that measuring a student teacher's performance in terms of behaviorally stated tasks serve four vital functions:

1) provides reference for selection of appropriate practice for supervisors and student teachers,
2) guides supervising teachers in systematic and accurate observation of teaching,
3) provides a continuum of criteria as a base for more precise evaluation, and
4) generates data for teacher education program improvement. (17)

Various state departments of education have felt strongly enough in the competency-based evaluation models that they have mandated the use of such a model for their student teachers. For example, the South Carolina legislature, in their Education Improvement Act, established a task force to develop an instrument to measure minimal teaching competencies. The five categories being assessed in their plan include planning, instruction, management, communication, and attitude. (18) The trend in many other states is toward more specificity in terms of measurable results in student teachers.

3. Humanistic Evaluation Model

Postman and Weingartner define a good school as one that moves away from factory-like processing procedures and toward more humanistic, individualized judgments. The idea is to make evaluation a learning experience. (19)

Advocates of the humanistic evaluation model for student teachers stress attitudes, open communication, genuineness, empathy, and warmth. Another emphasis of humanistic models of evaluation relates to the development of self and individual identity. (20) The use this model is an attempt to get student teachers to be more cognizant of students as persons rather than to learn to be masters of delivering content to an audience.

Arthur Combs, (21) dedicated advocate of humanism, relates the potential problems of humanistic education models. First, humanistic objectives are often general in nature and do not lend themselves to precise measurement. For example, evaluation of creativity is so multidimensional that accurate behavioral assessment is impractical. Also many humanistic objectives deal with intangibles such as attitudes, values, fears, and aspirations, all of which are difficult to measure.

Despite these potential drawbacks educators have recognized the values of humanistic forms of evaluation and have designed many procedures to formulate humanistic-type objectives, checklists, and data collection suggestions for cooperating teachers to utilize. These efforts toward an inclusion of humanistic forms of evaluation help to make the student teaching evaluation experience a more meaningful and lasting professional developmental period for the preservice teacher.

COMPARISON OF EVALUATION MODELS: CHARACTERISTICS AND STRENGTHS

Horizontal	Vertical	Humanistic
emphasis on applying and relating theory to practice	emphasis on mastery of specific competencies	assessment of intangible traits (creativity, empathy, warmth, openness, etc.)
need for self-evaluative input as a component to the final assessment	easy to assess because of its objective nature	highly individualized to produce more aware and sensitive teachers

Cooperating teachers, as well as student teachers, vary in philosophy, formality, and personality. The most appropriate model for evaluating any one student teacher must take into account these variables. Newport combined many of the previous models' philosophies when he recommended that cooperating teachers utilize a set of professional competencies for evaluation of student teaching, but individualize the list for each student teacher rather than using a standardized list. He also encouraged student teachers to identify many of their own criteria relevant to their preferred teaching styles. (22)

Every effort made in the evaluation of the student teacher should be qualitative with clear purpose and professional implementation. The evaluation model must also be flexible and open to include many valuable and meaningful aspects for the student teacher. The most important part of any model is the involvement of both the cooperating teacher and the student teacher in the entire process. This form of open communication will allow the "sting" of uncomfortable evaluations to dissipate into long term learning experiences.

THE BIG QUESTION!

"DOES HE REALLY MEASURE UP?"

PROBLEM ANALYSIS No. 31:   A Test of Patience

Doug, a new student teacher, teaches a
social studies lesson to the sixth grade class.
He describes the continent of Africa as the
largest continent in the Western hemisphere and
also spells the words "continent" and
"hemisphere" incorrectly on the blackboard.
Students are asked to copy the words and
definitions from the board. A student asks what
ocean surrounds Africa and Doug replies "I think
it is the Mediterranean." These inconsistencies
and glaring errors are not evident in his lesson
plan and you suspect that they occur because he
is nervous and hurrying through the lesson.
Perhaps he hasn't left time to think or check
possible choices so that the students (and Doug)
can figure out the right answers.

MAKING DECISIONS:

Do you stop the lesson and correct these
errors? Should you ask a specific question which
illustrates that a wrong answer has been offered?
Do you wait it out until the mistakes become
obvious to someone? Is there an alternative
action?

PROBLEM ANALYSIS No. 32:   When Is Enough Enough?

You are pleased with the progress of your
student teacher. However, you consciously expend
time and effort to evaluate strengths and

weaknesses in most lessons. One day your student teacher comments: "My friend Jenny's cooperating teacher said that she is confident of her ability and no longer writes daily comments for her teaching performance. When do you think that I will get to that place?"

MAKING DECISIONS:

What should you do to fulfill your responsibilities and not appear to be too overbearing? How should you respond to the actions of a fellow teacher who has "given up" on the daily evaluations?

PROBLEM ANALYSIS No. 33: PLEASING THE PRINCIPAL

Your principal's above all request is neatness in appearance for teachers. Your student teacher often wears blue jeans and sweaters to teach. He always looks neat and clean, but you know that the principal dislikes this kind of attire.

MAKING DECISIONS:

Would role would you adopt in this potential confrontation? Could the problem affect the administrator's evaluation of your student teacher?

PROBLEM ANALYSIS No. 34:   IS IT WORTH THE HASSLE?

Your   student teacher is overly sensitive to
any criticism or suggestions.   She begins to cry
with   every confrontation.   When you evaluate her
teaching   performance it is tempting to   overlook
weaknesses   and   avoid the inevitable tears which
would follow.

MAKING DECISIONS:

How   should   this   behavior   influence   your
evaluations, your   role   in conferencing, and the
final written evaluation for the institution?

Applying Ideas:

1. Select students to role play the following evaluation sessions:

a. Cooperating teacher must tell the student teacher that she will submit an "unsatisfactory" at midterm because of incomplete work.

b. The cooperating teacher will participate in a three way conference with the student teacher's college supervisor to explain dissatisfaction with the student teacher's academic grasp of French, his chosen content area and teaching field.

c. Cooperating teacher attempts to justify the grade of "B" to the student teacher who has completed all of the listed competencies successfully, but is somewhat lacking in performance of intangibles and hard to measure qualities such as creativity, enthusiasm, and warmth.

2. Ask students to work in pairs to develop a checklist of desired competencies that incorporates essential elements of the vertical, horizontal, and humanistic models. Ask them to identify which model each item represents.

3. Discuss the following remark made by a student teacher to a cooperating teacher. "If you were being graded instead of me, what do you think you would get for a final grade?" What are the implications of this question? How should a cooperating teacher answer? Is it appropriate to have a student teacher "grade" his cooperating teacher's performance? Why or why not?

NOTES: CHAPTER 8

1. Hershel D. Thornburg. Introduction to Educational Psychology. St. Paul, Minn.: West Publ. Co., 1984, p. 453.

2. John Hattie, Warwick Olphert, and Bruce Cole. "Assessment of Student Teachers by Supervising Teachers." Journal of Educational Psychology. v. 74 n. 5 (Oct. 1982), 776-85.

3. Jim Sweeney and Dick Manatt. "A Team Approach to Supervising the Marginal Teacher." Educational Leadership, April 1984, 25-27.

4. John Carl Williams and Wally S. Holmes. "Student Teacher Grades: What Do They Mean?" School and Community. 69:15, May 1983.

5. Gary A. Griffin. "Expectations for Student Teaching: What Are They and Are They Realized? Texas University: Austin: Research and Development Center for Teacher Education, April, 1983.

6. Williams and Holmes, op.cit.

7. Sharon F. O'Neal. "Supervision of Student Teachers: Feedback and Evaluation--Clinical Teacher Education and Preservice Skills," Texas University: Austin: Research and Development Center for Teacher Education, Feb., 1983.

8. Fanchon F. Funk. "The Influence of Feedback from Supervising Teachers on a Student Teaching Program." ERIC, 1978.

9. Jon J. Denton and Ebrahim Kazimi. "Relations Among Final Supervisor Skill Ratings of Student Teachers and Cognitive Attainment Values of Learners Taught by Student Teachers." Paper presented at Annual Meeting of the S.W. Educational Research Association, Austin, Tex., 1982.

10. John Hattie and others, op.cit.

11. Andrew Gitlin. "Horizontal Evaluation: An Approach to Student Teacher Supervision." Journal of Teacher Education. Sept./Oct. 1981 v.32 n.5, 47-50.

12. A.E. Wheeler and H.R. Knoop. "Self, Teacher, and Faculty Assessments of Student Teaching Performance." Journal of Educational Research. v 75 n.3 Jan/Feb. 1982, 178-181.

13. Andrew Gitlin, Rodney T. Ogawa, and Ernest Rose. "Supervision, Reflection, and Understanding: A Case for Horizontal Evaluation." Journal of Teacher Education v. 35 n .3 May/June 1984, 46-52.

14. Gitlin (1981) op.cit.

15. Maria Defino. "The Evaluation of Student Teachers." Texas University, Austin Tex.: Research and Development Center for Teacher Education, April, 1983.

16. Colden Garland. Guiding Clinical Experiences in Teacher Education. N.Y.: Longman, Inc., 1982.

17. C. Leland Smith and J. Truman Stevens. "A Criterion-Referenced Evaluation of Student Teachers in Science." School Science and Math. v.84 n.2 Feb., 1984, 125-135.

18. Chester R. Freeze. "The Length of Time Spent in Student Teaching as a Factor in Teacher Performance at Clemson University." Paper presented at AACTE, 1984.

19. Neil Postman and Charles Weingartner. How To Recognize A Good School. Bloomington, Ind.: Phi Delta Kappan Educational Foundation, 1973, p. 35.

20. Guy R. Lefrancois. Psychology for Teaching. Belmont, California: Wadsworth, Inc., 1982, 191-193.

21. Arthur W. Combs. "Assessing Humanistic Objectives: Some General Considerations." Humanistic Education: Objectives and Assessment. Washington, D.C.: Assoc. for Supervision and Curriculum Development, 1978.

22. John F. Newport. "Users Approve of a New Way to Evaluate Student Teachers." Clearinghouse. 55: 414-416. May, 1982.

Orienting Inquiry:

1.   How much variation in student teachers may I expect?

2.   What is the professional relationship expected to like between the college supervisor and the cooperating teacher?

3.   How important is the relationship between the cooperating teacher and the student teacher?

> "Student teaching may be defined as a complex intermingling of roles and institutions. Few, however, would dispute that the core of student teaching is the unique relationship which occurs between two persons-- the student teacher and the cooperating teacher."(1)

The Cooperating Teacher and Student Teacher

A student teacher may be competent in content mastery, skilled in methodology, and trained in evaluation procedures, but not know how to relate to people or how to assume the role of leadership necessary to be an effective teacher. You therefore have the task of establishing a positive relationship based on support and personal involvement. In this relationship the student teacher can develop interpersonal skills and learn to adjust to new and challenging situations. Remember that you will be requiring him to use capabilities he will exercise for the very first time. There is no easy formula in this adjustment process because each person approaches the relationship with individual goals, personality, background, and level of commitment to the experience.

You may encounter many types of personalities when working with student teachers. Jo Ann Taylor (1983) has grouped student teacher learners into three types: 1) the non-assertives, 2) the friendship seekers, and 3) the workers. "Non-assertives" have received the most written attention by researchers. These student teachers are passive in practice and show little excitement for teaching. They have difficulty with classroom management and are inconsistent in their treatment of students. "Friendship seekers" want children to like them, often at the expense of student gain in academic or social skills. These people have difficulty with discipline because they do not want to be considered mean by any child. The "workers" show initiative, react to needed improvements, and are resourceful for meeting individual needs. (2)

The overall characteristics of student teachers will determine which interpersonal strategies may be most productive. If the student teacher is generally passive and non-assertive, it will no doubt surface early in the experience. This type of student teacher may observe students with little interest in getting to know them. During conferences he may ask few or no questions regarding role expectations or requirements. While observing, he may hesitate to help with individual students, to grade papers, or to assist with extra-curricular activities.

Passive attitudes are difficult to change or challenge, but sometimes this withdrawn or apathetic behavior hides a fear of failure. It may be necessary to insist on a series of small, direct assignments which allow the student teacher to experience success. The process often is slow. If the student teacher does not assume responsibility for subsequent activities, you will be limited in what you can do. If he does not want a professional challenge, you cannot be expected to supply it. The student teacher who is generally apathetic and non-assertive needs guidance from the cooperating teacher in the form of written goals and specific dates for completion. For example, if detailed lesson plans are required one day prior to teaching and a plan is not submitted, the cooperating teacher is asking for problems if the student teacher is permitted to teach "off the cuff." We suggest that you do not confuse the terminology "suggestion" and "requirement" for this type of student teacher. Do not leave essential requirements open to interpretation by the student teacher. Concise and specific records of decisions, requirements, and results must be maintained. Your concerns and suggested techniques should be written and presented to the student teacher at the time of conference. In the periodic evaluation of progress and especially at the conclusion of student teaching, any questions of completion or satisfactory competence can be answered when you hold the recorded evidences at hand. Duplicates of statements should be periodically given to the college supervisor. It is fortunate that most non-assertives do respond to the positive and firm cooperating teacher. They accept guidance and welcome the chance to succeed if the help is fair, consistent, and offered with a sincere desire to promote professional competence.

The friendship seeker requires a different relationship and merits some special handling. This person is sometimes critical of the cooperating teacher's (or other teacher's) disciplinary methods and may attempt to portray himself as being fairer, more understanding, and truly empathetic. He may encourage students to use his first name, involve himself excessively in "kid" games, and permit unlimited excessive student freedom during instruction. The inconsistencies noted by children play havoc with established forms of discipline techniques. Any battle for control by popularity can be harmful and confusing for students.

In most cases "friendship seekers" are frustrated when achievement and test grades drop and general discipline breaks down and becomes unmanageable. It is the role of the cooperating teacher to institute a campaign within the conference sessions which will help the student teacher to reassess procedures and priorities. Together you can develop strategies which will promote a new environment for establishing relationships. The goal then can be to encourage mastery and competence, sometimes at the expense of "friendship." This potential loss, however, is sometimes offset by a new found respect.

The "workers" usually are enjoyable and beneficial to all persons they contact. They produce many types of units, creative lessons and interesting learning stations, find unique resource persons, and develop educational aids to stimulate enthusiasm for learning. The energetic student teacher usually is academically competent. Areas pinpointed for improvement generally are also recognized by the student teacher and suggestions are welcome. These are the "professionals" who periodically show the old dogs new tricks, demonstrate a creative twist on the lesson, or challenge model behavior and efforts. Both of you grow in this association. These are the student teachers who have the best chance to be excellent teachers and reflect credit on both the cooperating teacher and on the profession. It is not surprising to discover that their first offer for employment often is given by the principal or superintendent where they student taught.

The following list of suggestions is provided to you to maximize the opportunity for developing a positive relationship with student teachers:

--be a good listener.

--treat the student teacher as a peer and fellow authority figure in the presence of students and faculty.

--include the student teacher in many outside educational activities that are a part of your professional life (a night basketball game, dance, drama presentation, P.T.A., professional seminars, etc.)

--if a serious problem arises, discuss it immediately with your student teacher. It doesn't help him to learn if you attempt to "smooth it over" without involving his efforts.

--if possible, rather than correct errors made in the presence of students, list these on a memo card and save it for the conference discussion.

--make certain that conference discussions include recognition of progress, positive attitudes, or commendable performance.

--encourage early independence and responsibility as soon as appropriate, and increase these traits steadily throughout the experience.

--do not discuss specific student teaching problems with other teachers or outside personnel. If a concern merits attention, seek the help of the principal and/or the college supervisor.

--develop a professional and supportive argument when students openly criticize the student teacher and let you know they will "be glad to have you back." Students need to know that they also have a responsibility to help prepare new teachers.

Very few student teachers can maintain an equilibrium of confidence, self-concept, and emotional stability throughout the learning experience. Examine the following graph of a typical eight week experience. (Sharpe, 1970). Note that about half way through the experience many student teachers suffer a "low" in their mental outlook. There are many possible reasons for this pattern. They may include an increasing problem with discipline, establishing motivation, an unseemly amount of work, nervousness, frequent encounters with supervisors, new problems in evaluation, and often just plain fatigue. Usually this depression is followed by an increasing "up" that peaks by the end of student teaching. Discuss and predict patterns with your

147

student teacher. The experience and support may help to minimize or at least make his emotional highs and lows more understandable and endurable.

Graph-Highs and Lows of Student Teaching(3)

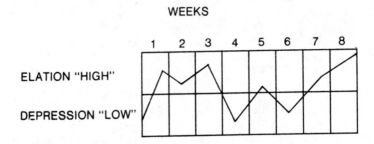

Most student teachers experience a variety of anxieties during the preparation period. Be alert and suggest remedies for these concerns in an attempt to promote the student teacher's self-concept and growth as a professional.

The Cooperating Teacher and the College Supervisor

Relationships between the college supervisor and the cooperating teacher vary in formality, frequency, and significance to the teacher preparation program. Frequent observations, after school visitations, two and three way conferences, and periodic three way evaluation activities require a fine tuned professional approach to the tasks at hand. Unfortunately, in some instances the relationship is no more than a quick stop and an occasional "Hello, how are things going? Any problems? See you later." This association does little to indicate support, involvement, or interest.

Opinions vary concerning the appropriate number and length of visitations by the college supervisor. Ideally, he should make weekly visits to each student teacher. During these observations, the college supervisor should critique and offer feedback so that the student teacher can plan effectively for future classes. Feedback should be both verbal and written. The supervisor should keep the cooperating teacher informed of the results of observations, evaluations, and recommendations.

The building of a productive professional relationship with the college supervisor depends on his accessibility. He should initiate the first meeting with the student teacher and you. The relationship also is affected by the level of competency of the student teacher. Student teachers who experience serious problems that might result in failure require the college supervisor to collect more data, attend more conferences, and work harder with the student teacher on specific problem areas. On the other hand, if the student teacher needs little guidance or professional instruction, the college supervisor's role may be less involved.

Researchers often have described the cooperating teacher's role to be the most vital in this three-dimensional relationship. However, the role of the college supervisor should not be underestimated. As the cooperating teacher, you can promote the relationship with the college supervisor by requesting three way conferences, soliciting advice, and sharing your progress reports. It is your responsibility to guarantee open communication and produce a feedback system that encourages help for the student teacher.

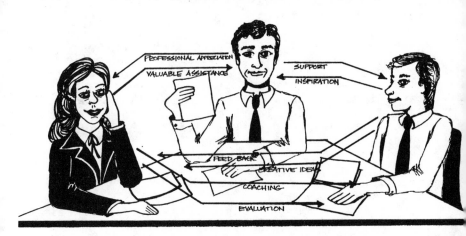

EFFECTIVE & PRODUCTIVE INTERACTION REQUIRES RESPECTFUL, DYNAMIC, PROFESSIONAL IMPUT, AND OPEN COMMUNICATION AMONG ALL THREE PARTIES.

INTERACTION

Another facet of the relationship between college supervisor and cooperating teacher is the collaboration needed to yield a final grade or competency measure for the student teacher. Controversy exists concerning this responsibility. Should the final evaluation be the role of the college supervisor or the cooperating teacher? Some researchers feel that the cooperating teacher should be responsible. "Seldom have we entrusted these master teachers with final decision making. Opportunity exists if the teacher education programs include training in clinical supervision for master teachers. Then university supervisors can get out of the public schools as student teacher supervisors to offer second opinions." (4) Whether the final evaluative decision belongs to the cooperating teacher or the college supervisor, or to both equally, it remains necessary for both persons to be aware of problems, progress, or specific achievements of the student teacher. This can be accomplished only through an on-going evaluation and open communication between the college supervisor and cooperative teacher.

The development of interpersonal skills, leadership, self-confidence, and sensitivity to the human condition are the key traits to successful and productive professional relationships with your student teacher and the college supervisor. It is interesting to note just how much of each trait results from learned behaviors on your part and that ironically, these are the very same traits you are charged with promoting in student teachers.

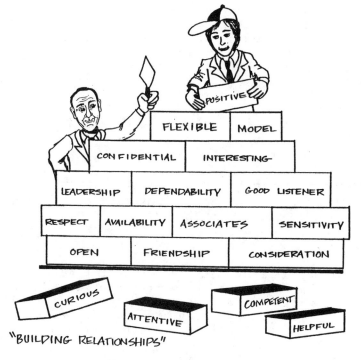

"BUILDING RELATIONSHIPS"

PROBLEM ANALYSIS No. 35:   CAUGHT UNAWARE

This week the student teacher has been planning to teach a small reading group. She is usually well-prepared and appears to work well in small group situations. During the follow-up conferences she is enthusiastic and shares experiences and ideas. Everything seems to be fine until you receive a shocking phone call from an irate parent. The parent reports that the student teacher has been discussing the separation of church and state with students and has told the students that they are not supposed to mention Christmas or any related activities during the school day.

MAKING DECISIONS:

Since you have a good relationship and can discuss things openly with your student teacher, what action seems to be the most appropriate in this situation? Do you confront other parents? students? the principal? Do you discuss the matter only with your student teacher? What seem to be the most effective answers?

PROBLEM ANALYSIS No. 36:   A CONFLICT OF TOLERANCE LEVELS

When you first met your student teacher, she was enthusiastic to begin the experience. She seemed well informed about the curriculum, teaching techniques, and planning. However, as she observes your teaching each day, she seems to become less interested. After several days of observing, you suggest that she begin to teach a small group and begin to plan for a science or social studies unit to teach to the entire class. Her enthusiasm appears to be minimal and she finally confesses that she would not be able to teach in such a permissive atmosphere. She insists that children must be quiet and doing seat work in order to learn.

MAKING DECISIONS:

What can you do to instill an enthusiasm in your student teacher? How can you bring your differences in style closer together so that she feels comfortable in working with your class?

PROBLEM ANALYSIS No. 37:   HANDLING "YOUR BIG MOUTH"

Larry, a student teacher of about four weeks, feels that he has a good relationship with you as his cooperating teacher. He feels that his conferences have been encouraging and he is gaining self-confidence in his teaching ability. One day, however, while passing by the teacher's lounge, he overhears you talking to some other teachers about him. You are describing many of his faults and general ineptness. Also you state that you don't think that you can help him and you don't know why the college sends you all the "duds." He confronts you with this information at the next conference session.

MAKING DECISIONS:

You now know that your mouth has gotten you in a mess. What should you do to help Larry? What statements should be made and to whom?

PROBLEM ANALYSIS No. 38: FORGETFUL FRED

Fred frequently displays an irresponsible forgetfulness. He left his jacket at school for three days following his first observation visit. He frequently misplaces his teaching manuals, loses student papers, and leaves materials such as ditto papers wherever last used. He lost a box of art supplies and every pen from my desk is missing. Fred's teaching seems to be satisfactory but this irresponsibility gets on my nerves and at times affects his performance as a teacher.

MAKING DECISIONS:

How do you deal with Forgetful Fred? Will a conference telling him of your dissatisfaction be adequate?

154

This morning the college supervisor observed your student teacher and had several comments for areas of needed improvement. The college supervisor discussed these areas with both the student teacher and you. During lunch, when the student teacher spoke with you and several other teachers, she was openly critical of the college representative and defensive to his comments. She stated that the comments were insignificant because he was a lousy teacher anyway.

MAKING DECISIONS:

How should you respond to such negative criticism of the college supervisor by your student teacher? Should the comments be ignored, reprimanded, or reported to the college?

1. As a group discussion, consider the cooperating teacher and student teacher whose personalities clash severely. Should the student teacher be reassigned in this case? Suggest alternatives, procedures, advantages, and disadvantages of such a reassignment.

2. As a take home assignment develop three approaches that you might use with a non-assertive or disinterested student teacher.

3. Discuss how you would approach the problem of a college supervisor who is disruptive to the learning process for both the student teacher and the students in his class during supervisory visitations. You basically disagree with the position that the college supervisor takes on many of the unpleasant interruptions and confrontations. (He tends to correct the student teacher during instruction.)

NOTES: CHAPTER 9

1) Jean Easterly, "Mutual Choice Placement-A Humanistic Approach to Student Teaching Assignments." ERIC, May, 1977.

2) Jo Ann Taylor. "A College Supervisor Speaks to Student Teachers." Kappa Delta Pi Record. v.20 n.1. Fall, 1983, 20-23.

3) Donald M. Sharpe. A Brief Guide to Secondary Student Teachers. Indiana State University. Terre Haute, Ind., 1970, p. 11.

4) Edward L. Miller. "Teacher Education: Pre-service and Inservice," Clearinghouse, v. 56, April, 1983, 364-367.

Orienting Inquiry:

---

1. What are the special problems that may occur with some student teachers?

2. What adjustments and remedies are suggested for highly personal or emotional situations?

3. What can I expect from the "average" student teacher?

4. Are problem student teachers the "exceptions or the rules?"

"Teacher education is over-regulated to a degree exceeded only, perhaps, in the nuclear industry. Yet the problem of poor teacher quality, which the regulations are aimed at preventing, grows continunally worse." (1)

Before you read about the potential problem student teachers, please be aware that you will not experience most of the problems discussed in this chapter. However, you need to be alert to possible conflicts or negative encounters with student teachers. When problems do occur they will affect you, the students in your class, and other school personnel. There are no single or easy solutions to many of the described concerns. Yet, it is important to examine multiple solutions or answers to the problems. Student teachers described in this chapter do exist. Most of the examples provided are real, not hypothetical. A prompt diagnosis of situations will help to reduce the tension and will

159

encourage immediate action to remedy problems.
Examine the following seven potential types of
problem student teachers. Try to critique ways
for handling a candidate with these traits in
your classroom situation.

PROBLEMS, PROBLEMS, PROBLEMS,

1. The Academically Deficient Student Teacher

Student teachers are entering a profession
which, in the opinion of the public, is
decreasing in respect, effectiveness, and
competence. Education majors, do in comparison
with other pre-professional majors, have slightly
lower standardized test scores. Reasons for

these lower scores vary, but the results are the same nevertheless. Unfortunately there are some education students who are minimally prepared although they have completed the requirements and are assigned to student teaching roles.

It is possible that as a cooperating teacher you will be asked to work with just such a person. In some cases, the missing skills for successful teaching can be acquired or improved with hard work, clear-cut strategies, and a heavy dosage of patience. In some cases, the student teacher is clearly "over his head" in one or more areas like spelling, grammar, content knowledge, organization, or the ability to relate to students. In these cases, you may choose to use a variety of observation techniques and session recordings which allow the student teacher the opportunity to recognize errors and accept suggested plans for remediation activities to remove deficiencies. Discovery of serious academic deficiencies makes it necessary to involve the college supervisor at an early date. Requests for the professor's observations and conferences should be accompanied by descriptions of the problem that you feel needs attention.

In a special case in which the student's academic background is so severely deficient that the student teacher cannot perform at a minimal level, it may be necessary to remove the candidate from the educational setting. Although state departments of education and higher education institutions are utilizing more rigorous screening devices and competency testing, this special case still may occur. Be prepared to express or exercise your professional judgment and take the steps necessary to protect both your students and the profession. Appropriate solutions should be evident if you collect and analyze adequate data, involve the college supervisor, and conduct frequent two and three way conferences in which written statements of the problem and descriptive analyses of teaching behaviors are presented for discussion. A student teacher's self analysis also should be incorporated into the three way conferences for subsequent evaluation and remedial actions.

You may be assigned an "underachiever" as a student teacher. In this case you may find yourself asking "How can I get this person to take the initiative, to be prepared for teaching, and to complete necessary work?" An obvious, but hardly comforting answer is that it isn't your responsibility to coax or coerce a student teacher into accepting his asssigned tasks. It is your job to spell out clear expectations. Do not add hidden surprises or last minute requests for work that were not supplied earlier. You can be a good listener and help with important problems, but you should not pull strings or overlook important requirements just to "get him through." If the student teacher is not ready for the responsibility of planning and teaching, he may need to reassess his priorities and pursue another career. He may feel that the demands are not in line with the rewards. If this is the case, you may be saving someone from a necessarily short and anguish-filled career in education. It also should be noted that other student teachers may express strong desires to teach, but cannot improve in achievement. They should be evaluated in a similar objective and open manner. If they don't measure up, they should find another area of interest as well. No "guilt feelings," "inadequacies," or "failures" are in line for the cooperating teacher. Simply stated, "You did your professional best, but the student teacher didn't, couldn't, or wouldn't."

2. Student teachers with Excessive Emotional or Personal Problems

As mentioned earlier the anxiety levels are high at the beginning of the experience and decline gradually by the end of student teaching. Some student teachers, however, experience excessive stress and frustration throughout the total experience. Low self-esteem and depression may influence the student teacher to withdraw, give up, or endure to a final failure. Emotional and personal problems can be expected and often at best you may be left to "treat the symptoms." For example, if the student teacher feels that he is not liked or that he is not creative you might attempt to determine if he has enough data to justify these feelings. Then try to work out alternative strategies, better assessment methods, or new approaches to handle the deeply felt anxiety. Even if the problem is only an imagined or exaggerated one, it should be discussed privately but openly in your conferences. Often stated worries are an expression of a need for support or approval. It is difficult to determine the difference between the effects of little self-confidence and those effects brought on by too little experience to know the difference among "poor," "average," "good" or "excellent."

Student teachers may show their anxieties in many ways. Occasionally an over-zealous or worried student teacher may work so hard at "winning over the students" that he undermines your efforts in uncomplimentary ways. It may appear that his "ego-centered logic and vicious intent" combine to produce a person who wants to take over and seek the leadership of the classroom. If such behaviors occur in your student teacher, you should relate your perceptions to him as soon as they surface and re-explain the expectations for a professional team relationship. It is possible that the student teacher does not understand his own motives and/or that you have overreacted to his desire to be the "best." In either case the needs to protect the relationship and to respect each other's roles are essential. If no adjustments are made by the student teacher and the problem persists, further action should be taken in cooperation with the college supervisor. You should never accept or tolerate unprofessional behavior. Immediate attention is required so that small "mistakes or misdirected actions" do not become large issues.

Another emotional situation may result in the undesirable development of a relationship between the student teacher and your students. Attraction and mutual romantic interests negate the age gap differences between mature pupils and immature student teachers. Romantic involvements and idolizing affections can lead to serious problems. The prepared and mature student teacher will handle invitations, flirting, or teasing in a sensible, non-active and low-key manner. This approach leaves both parties with self-worth and respect. The immature or inexperienced student teacher, however, may be flattered by the attention received. If you suspect a potential problem, offer suggestions to help the student teacher handle the situation. These suggestions might include the need for direct communication with the involved student, subtle avoidance behavior that discourages further overtures, or even extinction actions to ignore and dissipate the advances of the student. In all cases your advice must include clear arguments against encouragement, further involvement, or excessive interest in the student as a "special friend." Do not allow embarassing situations to develop if at all possible. Call in a third party (college supervisor or school administrator) if you need the support to influence professional behavior on the part of your student teacher. If no action is taken until a parent complaint is filed, you may be in serious trouble professionally.

Personal problems generated by the student teacher's family or close peers obviously cannot be solved at school by the cooperating teacher. However you can be an empathic and supportive listener. Encourage discussion and help the student teacher to restate the problem and use it as a model for similar instances that he might expect in the future. Together, make an effort to keep personal problems (yours and his) isolated from the teaching situation so that they do not affect the learning processes or curricular activities in adverse ways. The cooperating teacher should be a friend and counselor as well as model, facilitator, and evaluator during these problem times.

Morgan found that teachers who rated high on empathy and understanding were rated high on teaching performance as well. (2) This finding seems to suggest that by directing energies away from personal problems and toward concern for others' problems, the teacher actually may enhance his own teaching performance. As mentioned earlier, the model that you set in handling the problem for the student teacher should serve as an example of how the student teacher may use the same techniques, empathy, and support for problems found among his students.

3. Student Teachers with Financial Worries

Money worries can affect the young teacher's performance. During student teaching pressures increase if the student must manage a tight budget during a semester of high expense and no income. Lunch money, expected dinner meetings, costs of "professional" clothing, and daily supplies make financial worries acute for some student teachers. Many individuals may be comfortable communicating these concerns to you, but others may be too embarassed to say anything. If you suspect that finances are a worry, you may help to find some relief for the problem. Your understanding and concern could be accompanied by some support for supplies from the school funds.

It is possible, on the other hand, to have a student teacher who spends too much money on preparations and supplies by trying to "win over" students with surprises. You will need to address over-extending practices with sound advice and suggestions for more conservative actions.

4. Student Teachers who Find it Difficult to Adjust to a New Environment

Student teachers who are comfortable with the college atmosphere of friends, teachers, classroom work, and party time may find the move to public school routine with its own population, rules, expectations, and responsibilities a difficult adjustment. The nature of the cooperating teacher's approach to the welcome and orientation of the student teacher can help in this transition. It is important to include many introductions to friends and fellow staff members. Also supply a list of the faculty and staff, provide basic hints for survival (limit the threats and warnings), and involve the student teacher early in current school events and functions. If you help your student teacher begin to feel like a professional associate, you can speed up the adjustment and identification as a peer. The transition to the classroom setting is a real problem for some student teachers. It is therefore not surprising to find that researchers report in studies of education majors as preservice teachers that the major adjustment problems are listed in four areas:

-- orientation to teaching (lack of lesson preparation, understanding of pupils' behavior, etc.)
-- understanding the partnership of teaching (who does what?: the student teacher, cooperating teacher, or college supervisor)
-- professionalism and the related responsibilities
-- attitudes toward commitment and skills (doing necessary errands). (3)

Most of these problem areas fade with experience and positive support. By being prepared you can anticipate the adjustments necessary to make the total learning experience for the student teacher much less stressful.

5. Student Teachers Who Have Trouble Adjusting to Multi-cultural and Economic Differences

To prepare student teachers with well-rounded multi-cultural experiences, many institutions place their teacher education students in situations quite different from their own personal socio-economic or cultural backgrounds. A college student with strong ties to a well educated family and from an upper-middle class economic and social association may find an assignment in a school with a population of economically depressed students, or another situation in which the parent population holds a low expectancy for school work beyond the sixth grade. Another adjustment difficulty for some student teachers is the realization that over 50 percent of the class population are from divorced or one parent families. Many of these situations can produce a kind of culture shock and can affect the adjustment process.

It is not an easy task to work within the situations described, but open communication initiated by you can help to remove anxiety, promote understanding, and provide alternative approaches. Discussion of each effort can help to facilitate adjustment, and allow the student teacher to realize a need and a utility for his abilities.

6. Student Teachers who Worry About Student Acceptance

An often expressed concern of student teachers is the manner in which they are accepted by the students. In some cases classes are not enthusiastic about welcoming a newcomer as their instructor. Lack of acceptance, overextending friendships, or failure to understand the teacher's role can result in confrontation and disagreement. Maintaining control of classroom order and discipline can become entangled with personal problems and adjustments can be difficult.

The student teacher who seeks acceptance may fraternize with students in an attempt to become "one of the gang." He may choose to spend outside school time in the company of students. Along with increased familiarity and "friendships," informal approaches to teaching may develop. These techniques are inappropriate and the professional respect needed as a teacher to promote responsible learning may be sacrificed.

Compliment the student teacher's concern and demonstrated empathy for students, but stress the need for respect, the need to be a role model, and the overall responsibilities of a "good" teacher. You also need to explain how informal approaches can result in major discipline problems. Try to redirect the student teacher's activities toward developing respect through effective teaching, comprehensive planning, and the establishment of working relationships with other members of the faculty.

7. Students with Problems Adjusting to Professional Roles

It usually is not possible to become a professional educator by coursework study alone. The student teaching experience under the direction of a sensitive, empathetic, and knowledgeable cooperating teacher can produce a model professional experience. However, you may meet the student teacher who has all the answers for everything, even before the questions are recognized. The student teacher/cooperating teacher relationship usually suffers from this approach. It is fortunate that the young person with this attitude can improve during the experience. If the student teacher resists your help and alternative suggestions, it may be advisable to allow some educational data to accumulate as the student teacher instructs in the manner she alone prefers. Keep notes and accurate data during the observations. In conference, turn the data interpretation over to the student teacher and call for her to evaluate each lesson. Appear ready to challenge misinterpretation and do point out the facts, but if she fails to see large mistakes or the pitfalls which surface, you may need to guide her to identify those which need improvement. Hold off suggestions or corrections until the student teacher perceives that she needs the help and can get it if she asks.

Professional attitudes also may be influenced by problems with drug use, alcohol abuse, theft, or socially unacceptable life style behaviors. These problems will affect professional relationships and may require outside help or counseling. Special problems like these add tremendous burdens and in some cases legal responsibilities for the cooperating teacher. If there is any chance that a problem could influence in an adverse way classroom procedure or conduct, involve legal authorities, reflect negatively on the school or on the teacher education program, immediate positive action is your responsibility. It may be easy to overlook or ignore the problem, but it is best to share your concern with the college supervisor and arrange for an immediate three way conference. Determine the appropriate next step (additional input from administration and the local authorities or the need for professional counseling session). At the conclusion of the meeting make certain that an agreement is reached. Be sure that the student teacher is committed to the discussion and to any agreements or contracts. Be certain to follow due process throughout the entire situation. (See Legal Issues, Chapter 13).

Is There No End to Problems?

The numerous problem areas discussed seem to suggest that every teacher education candidate demonstrates some inabilities or some weaknesses. Be reassured that many student teachers do not encounter any significant problems. We have found that most education students are mature, competent, enthusiastic, and well-adjusted individuals who love teaching, children, and the responsibilities that accompany the job description. Most experiences with student teachers are enjoyable, exciting, and result in memorable professional associations and lasting friendships.

Although some student teachers do have problems, most of these can be corrected with intelligent action, guidance, and patience. The real challenge seems to revolve around a professional association starting with general assumptions about backgrounds and abilities. Further challenge is encountered when you guide them progressively through a series of self educative experiences that may serve to unleash their finest efforts. When they wear the true title of "teacher" you know that you were a necessary contributor. But, then don't we try to do the very same thing with every child we teach each day? If you are successful with student teachers, you earn an honored second level title--"a teacher of teachers."

PROBLEM ANALYSIS NO. 40: NEWS YOU DIDN'T WANT TO KNOW

Ben is doing an outstanding job of planning, presenting, and evaluating students in your high school classes. He is enthusiastic and responds positively to suggestions. His social life has never been a part of any of your discussions with him. On Monday morning three eager seniors are anxious to tell you that they saw Ben at a party where he was smoking marijuana and drinking heavily. The students ask you what you plan to do about the situation.

MAKING DECISIONS:

Can you ignore the students' report? Would you confront the student teacher with this information? What action would you take in the best interest of everyone? Is it your responsibility to speak with the college supervisor? the principal? the boy's parents? How do you respond to the students who reported the incident and asked for your action?
How would you like this incident to affect Ben's teaching career?

PROBLEM ANALYSIS No. 41: STUDENT TEACHING COMES IN SECOND PLACE

Beth's overall college grades are low. You have learned that she shouldn't have been permitted to student teach because she did not have the required grade point average. Problems begin to surface during her first week with you. She says that she loves children and wants to teach, but cautions you that she has little time to prepare because of many unrelated commitments. She fails to have lesson plans ready, grade or return student papers within reasonable time, or prepare learning materials when needed. When challenged by you she will work all night if necessary to catch up on previous oversights and will come in prepared the following day. Soon, however, her work begins to slip and she repeats the pattern until threatened or challenged by you again.

MAKING DECISIONS:

Under what conditions would you excuse assignments? At midterm grading would you give a low grade? If you think that Beth can make a good teacher, how would you go about getting a total commitment?

PROBLEM ANALYSIS No. 42: THE STUDENT TEACHER LOSES RESPECT

Sheila is doing an excellent job of planning, presenting, and following up her lessons. The students seem to like her. She organizes many fun learning activities and does not depend on dull workbooks.

However, she does have some problems being assertive and enforcing the rules. The students have picked up on this weakness and some are not listening, others are doing "their own thing," and in general are not being respectful. She spends much time repeating directions or reprimanding the students for not listening.

This problem distracts from the lesson and interrupts the students who are being attentive. As a cooperating teacher it is difficult to ignore the worsening situation.

MAKING DECISIONS:

What appropriate suggestions or actions should you take with Sheila? How long should you wait before you take action?

PROBLEM ANALYSIS No. 43:   NEED FOR A CLOSER LOOK

The student teacher has just given a social studies test. You were not in the room when the test was given. When you examine the test papers, three students who seldom receive higher than a "D" grade scored as high or higher than the regular four or five "A" students in your class. You know that the three surprise students were not attentive to the student teacher when she presented the material.

One of your students approached you and explained that she saw students cheating, but that she was sure that the student teacher did not see them. Your student teacher is beaming and states her pride in the efforts shown by these three students.

MAKING DECISIONS:

Do you tell the student teacher the news of the students cheating or do you let her feel successful in motivating them? What would be the consequences of both solutions?

Applying Ideas:

1. Have students write two hypothetical case studies of special problems that were not discussed in this chapter. Encourage them to read the problems to the class and ask others to suggest ways that the problems may be resolved.

2. For each of the special problems identified in the chapter, indicate the degree that you feel competent to advise, direct, counsel, or instruct a student teacher with such a problem. Are some categories of problems easier to deal with than others?

NOTES: CHAPTER 10

1) W. Timothy Weaver. "Solving the Problem of Teacher Quality, Part 2." <u>Phi</u> <u>Delta</u> <u>Kappan.</u>, Nov., 1984 v.66 n.3, p. 185-188.

2) Sharon R. Morgan. "An Illustrative Case of High Empathy Teachers," <u>Humanistic</u> <u>Education</u> <u>and</u> <u>Development.</u> June, 1984, v. 22 n. 4, p. 143-148.

3) Jane H. Applegate and Thomas J. Lasley. "Cooperating Teachers' Problems with Preservice Field Experience Students," <u>Journal</u> <u>of</u> <u>Teacher</u> <u>Education.</u> March/April, 1982, v.33, n.2, p. 15-18.

11 Discipline and Classroom Management Problems

Orienting Inquiry:

---

1. How do you help a student teacher conquer the natural fears of controlling student behavior?

2. Why is a working knowledge of behavior modification, assertive discipline, reality therapy, and low profile classroom control necessary for a cooperating teacher?

3. What advice do you give to a student teacher who needs to develop effective management techniques?

"For more than half a century surveys have identified discipline as the primary concern of prospective and beginning teachers." (1)

The one major problem identified by all student teachers involved the development of effective management and discipline techniques. Researchers clearly have identified that the greatest area of stress during the student teaching semester is found in the area of managing discipline and student behavior. (2) Purcell and Seiferth, in their survey of student teacher perceptions, also found that the item of greatest difficulty for student teachers was the handling of discipline problems. (3) Henry found that discipline was the major problem encountered by student teachers regardless of the degree of preparation. (4) Lane and Morrow, in a broad survey of student teachers, cooperating teachers, and college supervisors, found that the area of most concern listed by each was discipline and classroom control. (5)

Sweeney and Manatt, who obtained data from more than 750 principals, could define clearly the "marginal teacher" as one who appears to have sufficient command of subject matter, but whose lack of classroom management skills gets in the way of student learning. (6) All of these studies emphasize the importance of appropriate discipline and management skills in the job of a student teacher.

Classroom management refers to the processes and provisions that are necessary to create and maintain environments in which teaching and learning can occur. A person who enters teaching expecting only to instruct students has an unrealistic vision of the job at hand.

Many student teachers do have an unrealistic (or perhaps uninformed) view of classroom discipline as they begin to teach. Often they feel that the cooperating teacher places too much emphasis on discipline techniques just to maintain order. Brumfield and Leonard, in their study, asked student teachers to rank the ten most important teacher characteristics before and then after the student teaching semester. The most significant switch occurred in the rank of "managing discipline problems." At the onset this area ranked in fourth place, but moved to first place as the single most important characteristic for the effective teacher. (7)

What can cooperating teachers do to minimize the interactions that promote discipline problems in the student teachers' experience? It is of foremost importance that you demonstrate the management techniques that are expected of an effective role model. Utilize and even exaggerate strategies which work and then discuss them with your student teacher. Inexperience may not let him understand why you use a particular method or approach but in discussion a rationale and way to promote better managment can be conveyed to the new teacher.

Also it is helpful to list specific techniques at an early conference before the student teacher attempts to teach. He then can see you use some of the suggestions and decide early which strategies he wants to attempt. For example, he should know beforehand what to do when John throws a pencil across the room or Sandra tells him that she doesn't have to listen to him because he is "only a student teacher." You might propose several role playing scenarios which offer practice and promote discussion. Remind the student teacher that the ultimate goal should be self-discipline on the part of each student. Techniques used should be designed to promote this primary objective.

It also will be instructive if you develop a series of classroom interaction anecdotes or problem analyses on index cards from your own experiences that could serve periodically as homework assignments or conference discussion topics for the student teacher. Add a question of procedure, of proper judgment, or how to establish values or make decisions in a way similar to the assignments of the problem analyses you have been asked to discuss in this textbook.

Management Techniques

One key to successful teaching is the ability to adapt and be creative and flexible in meeting each plan or objective. While a student teacher may accept and use a particular disciplinary technique for all in the class, individuals will, over a time, respond differently to various ideas. Help him to see that not all students will react in the same manner to the same techniques and that some methods, therefore, are not sufficient to meet all requirements. One must be adaptable and willing to try several approaches in an attempt to find the most appropriate strategy for each situation and for each individual. Encourage your student teacher to share successess and failures with you as he tries various techniques.

Four commonly used discipline models are presented in an abbreviated form so that they may be useful in a discussion of strategies for the student teacher. Combinations and applications of techniques should be encouraged.

Discipline Model No. 1: Behavior Modification

Behavior modification is the attempt to change observable and measurable responses through reinforcement, consequences that increase the likelihood of a favorable behavior reoccurring. Students vary from each other and even within themselves depending on the situation. Therefore the effects of reinforcement must vary. (8) A common classroom application of behavior modification is the popular use of positive reinforcement, a strategy to bring about the desired behavior through the use of appropriate reinforcers. Extrinsic (external) reinforcers may include verbal or written praise, grades, stars, privileges, tokens, food, candy, or a physical pat on the back. Teachers can guide and encourage learning experiences to create another kind of reinforcement, known as instrinsic (internal) reinforcement, or an individual self-satisfaction. This is a harder task to develop with students, but becomes a lasting accomplishment when effective. Positive reinforcement in general is an excellent method for bringing about the desired changes in students.

Another frequently used classroom application of behavior modification is the process known as extinction which involves the elimination of undesired behavior through the withdrawal of reinforcement. It is often the acknowledgement, the laughter, or the reprimand that encourages a student to continue undesirable behavior. Through patient ignoring of the behavior by the teacher and the class, the undesired behavior usually is diminished or extinguished.

Punishment is another behavior modification technique utilized frequently in classrooms. Punishment is any act that brings about pain or dissatisfaction to the recipient. It can include verbal or written disapprovals, low marks, deprivation of privileges, or paddling. The technique of punishment is criticized widely, but it is commonly used.

Thornburg lists six reasons why punishment, especially when compared to positive reinforcement, is not as effective as a classroom technique. Punishment:

1) controls behavior for a limited time only.
2) does not teach an alternative response and does not show students appropriate behavior.
3) is upsetting to the student, the teacher, and the entire class.
4) causes counteraggression as students plot how to "get even."
5) promotes the technique of punishment as a model for imitation.
6) causes withdrawal, both mentally and physically. (the student may avoid school or interaction with teachers and/or students). (9)

Discuss the application of punishment techniques with your student teacher. Have him provide specific weaknesses of the technique when used with particular students. There may be times when no other method seems to be appropriate, but the message should be that punishment is only one of several alternatives. As such it should be used sparingly and as a last resort.

Discipline Model Number 2:   Assertive Discipline

Lee Canter, the developer of the technique known as assertive discipline, states that a teacher must respond actively to a student's inappropriate behavior by communicating clearly the disapproval of the behavior. The teacher then should provide a precise explanation of what the child must do. The teacher must be "in charge" of the class and inform all students of the consequences of inappropriate behavior. Canter advocates a consistent plan which must be followed in every situation where a student's behavior is inappropriate. He designs a multi-

step plan to follow for subsequent misbehaviors
by the same child. The teacher should : 1)
write a child's name on the board for the first
misbehavior, 2) place a checkmark beside the name
for the second offense which automatically means
that the student owes 15 minutes of time, 3)
place a second checkmark beside the name for the
third offense, which means 30 minutes is owed,
4) call home upon the third checkmark to talk
with parents about inappropriate behavior, and 5)
organize administrative conferences for any
further offenses. Canter also stresses heavy
emphasis on positive rewards when students are
behaving appropriately. (10)

If your student teacher would like to try a
modified form of assertive discipline she should
develop the plan with the students and write and
post the list in the room so that each student is
aware of the discipline procedures. You may need
to monitor the system to assure that the student
teacher is consistent in carrying out the plan.
Without careful planning the system can become
completely punitive. Effort must be extended to
equalize the system with rewards and positive
actions.

Discipline Model Number 3:   Reality Therapy

A primary objective must include the
development of responsible behavior among
students. It is a job of teachers, therefore,
to help students to become aware of problems or
behaviors which prevent responsible conduct.
Identification of these problems and the
development of new and acceptable behavior form
the basis for the reality therapy techniques
developed by William Glasser.

He suggests extensive use of classroom
meetings so that students can express problems
publicly and explore needed solutions as a group.
Glasser's system tries to produce lasting changes
in the students' behavior. There is much in
Glasser's system that teachers find attractive--
student responsibility, behavior as choice,
reasonable consequences tied to behavior, and a

focus on the student's value commitment to better behavior.

There are, however, limitations to the use of this approach. It is a time-consuming system and can disrupt the cognitive lessons. Also it is nearly impossible to deal with more than one student problem at a time, and too often there are several problems which happen simultaneously. (11) Another problem may be the lack of experience in handling the "open" discussion sessions. An inexperienced teacher may let the situation get away from him and eventually do more damage than good in resolving the problem.

Discipline Model Number 4: Low Profile Classroom Control

Carl Rinne suggests that one answer to effective classroom control is a low-profile approach which "focuses student attention directly on lesson content without unnecessary distractions." He maintains that conventional (high profile) classroom controls distract student attention away from lesson content. The "Johnny, you turn around and pay attention," statements attract the entire class toward wondering what John was seeing in the first place.

Usually low-profile control is nearly unnoticed by students. The teacher inserts students' names at random into the lesson content itself. ("All of you, including Ann, Johnny, Bruce, and Sarah, look at the graph at the bottom of page 36.") This approach allows the lesson to proceed smoothly, pulling Johnny back to attention without embarassment or even an awareness that he is being controlled. Low-profile classroom teachers also move around to all parts of the room and seldom use the podium or desk as a "control center." Thus, they manage to visit all trouble spots along the route. (12)

Most student teachers feel comfortable implementing low-profile techniques. The benefits of this system force the teacher to think about the positive approaches that can be used and the need for punitive repercussions and conflicts become less necessary and important.

It is important that each behavioral category be discussed with and attempted by the student teacher. She should be aware of the benefits and the problems promoted by each of her actions. Discuss individual situations and encourage the student teacher to predict outcomes if alternative actions had been applied.

Survival Tactics to Share with Your Student Teacher

From a nearly endless list of suggestions for help to design a constructive disciplinary approach, the following set of pointers are presented. These survival skills may serve as a guide and reminder of teacher behaviors that promote attention and positive reaction from students. Suggestions like these should be included in a student teacher's handbook. Each reommendation should be discussed in conference sessions along with specific examples of how and when to use each.

1. Be consistent in your approach.

It is human nature to react differently to different students with similar behavioral offenses. You must use the same standards for each student.

2. Keep students busy in a constructive way.

A common cause for misbehavior is an excess of idle time or tasks which seem to have no other function than to "keep 'em busy." Students should be motivated at their individual levels with challenging work. Planning for worthwhile and interesting activities is time-consuming, but results and the reduction of tension are worth every effort.

3. Be organized and prepared.

Students of all ages sense disorder and confusion on the part of the teacher. Your student teacher should be encouraged to plan carefully and to have additional activities prepared if the time planned for is not needed. Disorganization on the part of a student teacher will encourage a disorganized, chaotic, and frustrating environment.

4. State a limited number of rules and discuss these with students.

A common mistake made by student teachers is to present too many major rules and punishments that usually are not followed. There is always a student who is curious to find out early just how serious the new student teacher really is. To avoid this confrontation, discuss with the students a plan for maintaining acceptable behavior. Students, if given the chance to be included, will react in a responsible manner, will be harder on themselves, and will accept some of the duties for helping the student teacher to succeed.

5. Have a sense of humor.

Students need to know that you are approachable and human. Laughter and fun are an important part of education. Rogers (1984) adds that "the strong, healthy personality with a well-developed sense of humor is much more likely to be able to cope successfully with adversity. Humor belongs in the classroom for what it teaches us and for its own sake." (13)

6. Follow through on statements made to students.

It is easy for a student teacher to threaten. Don't make threatening statements such as "you will lose privileges," "I'll send a note to the principal," or "I will call your parents" unless you plan to carry them out. Forewarnings made without any follow through diminish the student teacher's respect and reduce his authority. Think carefully before making threatening statements.

7. Move about so that you can associate and relate to all students.

Don't stay with one group for an extended period or with your back to the class. Move completely around and through the class so that you always are near and can glance frequently to see how things are proceeding.

<u>8.</u> <u>Vary</u> <u>your</u> <u>teaching</u> <u>style.</u>
Flexibility, creativity, and variety of teaching techniques will keep students interested, and minimize potential discipline problems.

<u>A</u> <u>Need</u> <u>for</u> <u>Confident</u> <u>Leadership</u>

There is no easy way to maintain a well-managed class. If there were, the anxiety over discipline would not be the major worry of student teachers. It may be comforting, however, to learn that the anxiety concerning student discipline and behavior decreases with the student teacher's progress in his experience. Kremer and Kurtz state that the perceptions that student teachers have about having control over their environment are critical to them. (14) As they become more confident in the effective use of management techniques, their perceptions will help to give them the courage to assert the leadership necessary for survival.

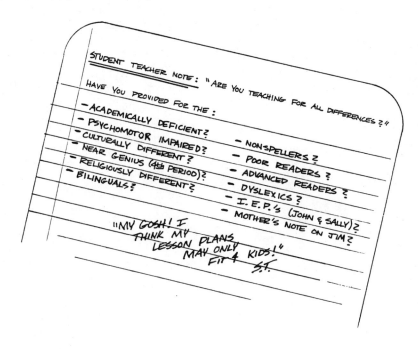

The cooperating teacher plays an essential role in aiding the student teacher to gain control over the teaching environment and to develop expertise and confidence in classroom management techniques. You must extend to the student teacher the idea that "weak leadership is likely to produce increased discipline problems, and strong leadership is likely to reduce them. (15)

PROBLEM ANALYSIS No. 44:   A TIME THAT TRIES MEN'S SOULS

One third grade class contains five boys who manage to keep the class "in an out of control environment" nearly every day. The classroom teacher and principal have tried numerous disciplinary tactics, but to date nothing works. The physical education teacher and a new student teacher will have the class for two hours of instruction each week.

MAKING DECISIONS:

As the cooperating teacher, how would you approach the conference on maintaining discipline? If a regular classroom teacher and principal have almost no control of the class, can a student teacher be expected to succeed? Would you even let the student teacher try to work with this class? Should you suggest the problem as a challenge?

PROBLEM ANALYSIS No. 45: WHAT IS GOOD DISCIPLINE?

Mrs. Jones was pleased with Sue's student teaching performance to date. She discusses the discipline guidelines with Sue, but gave her the option to trying her own approach. Sue followed Mrs. Jones' procedures for several weeks and then began to relax the rules. The new approach was successful with the majority of the class, but several students do not appear to be on task. They are somewhat noisy and Mrs. Jones feels that this is disruptive. She expresses her concern, but Sue does does not consider the students' behavior as disruptive. The apparent lack of "on task time," however, has not resulted in lower achievement scores for any of the students in daily or unit evaluation.

MAKING DECISIONS:

Should Mrs. Jones ask Sue to tighten the discipline and for what reasons? Should she allow Sue independence and freedom to pursue the more "liberal approach?" Should she stress the importance of "on task time" and the problems that can arise if everyone is not doing the assignment in a quiet and respectful manner?

PROBLEM ANALYSIS No. 46: WHERE'S BRIAN?

You are very confident of Claudia's discipline techniques with your kindergarten class and therefore feel comfortable leaving the room for short periods of time while she is teaching. After lunch one day, Claudia begins a lesson with the class in a large circle. She completes the lesson and has the children return to their seats. It is then that she discovers that one of the quiet boys, Brian, is missing. She sends a frantic message to you for help. You search the lunchroom, playground, bathroom, and library, but have no luck in finding Brian.

MAKING DECISIONS:

What steps should you take at this moment? How should you include Claudia in your actions with the administration and the parents? After the problem is solved (Brian had a stomach ache and he slipped off to home without telling anyone), what advice, consolation, or reprimands do you lay on to Claudia?

PROBLEM ANALYSIS No. 47: "SOME MIDDLE SCHOOL STUDENTS ARE NOT NAIVE"

Mark is an energetic middle school student teacher. One day, while alone getting materials ready in the gym for a special activity, he hears some noises behind the bleachers. When he investigates, he finds two eighth graders in an inappropriate sexual encounter. The students are shocked and frightened when discovered, and plead for Mark not to tell anyone because their parents would "kill them." Mark comes to you with the statement, "Perhaps I shouldn't go any further with these students, but I honestly don't know what to do. What would you do if you had found them?"

MAKING DECISIONS:

What is your responsibility in this situation? How do you respond to Mark's dilemma? What professional actions should you take?

PROBLEM ANALYSIS No. 48: "IT'S A JUNGLE AT TIMES!"

Louise, a secondary student teacher, is in the hall when a female student uses extremely profane explitives to another female student. The student then begins to hit and scratch the other. Louise steps in to break up the fight. You arrive on the scene just as one of the girls smacks Louise in the face and tears off down the hall. Louise is near tears from the hurt and the humiliation, and perhaps the realization that at times school is a jungle.

MAKING DECISIONS:

What immediate action should you undertake? How should you handle the discussion with Louise?

PROBLEM ANALYSIS No. 49: "THE KIDS ACT UP ONLY WHEN YOU'RE IN THE ROOM"

Mary appears to be having management problems with your sixth grade students. She asks them to do tasks, but they ignore her and continue to talk and to be disruptive. Finally, in desperation, she tells them to put heir heads on their desks, but none of them do. In your conference with her, Mary tells you that the students only act up when you are in the room. She explains that they are in perfect control and are respectful when she has them to herself. You find this difference in perception difficult to believe.

190

MAKING DECISIONS:

How do you determine the disruptive level or the amount of respect shown while you are absent from the room? If you do find that there is no major difference in control no matter who is in the room, what would you do next?

Applying Ideas:

1. Assign written case studies of potential discipline situations that student teachers may encounter. Share these with the class to obtain ideas for solutions.

2. Have students select a list of management procedures that they would feel comfortable using. Ask them to indicate how they might attempt to get the student teacher to practice these techniques.

3. Select the management techniques which (with modifications) would work most effectively with adult groups. What do you notice about the leadership roles as a teacher, as a teacher of adults, and as a teacher of teachers?

1) Thomas J. Coates and Carl E. Thorensen.
"Teacher Anxiety: A Review with
Recommendations," Review of Educational Research
(Spring, 1976), p. 164.

2) J.E. Morris and G.W. Morris. "Stress in
Student Teaching," Action in Teacher Education.
2:4 Fall, 1980, p. 57-62.

3) Thomas D. Purcell and Bernice B. Seiferth.
"Tri-State Survey of Student Teachers." College
Student Journal. 16: 27-29. Spring, 1982.

4) Marvin Henry. "The Effect of Increased
Exploratory Field Experiences Upon the
Perceptions and Performance of Student Teachers."
Action in Teacher Education. v. 5 n. 1-2, p. 66-
70. Spring/Summer 1983.

5) John M. Lane and John E. Morrow.
"Instructional Problems of Student Teachers:
Perceptions of Student Teachers, Supervising
Teachers, and College Supervisors." Action in
Teacher Education. v.5 n.1-2, p. 71-78.
Spring/Summer, 1983.

6) Jim Sweeney and Dick Manatt. "A Team
Approach to Supervising the Marginal Teacher."
Educational Leadership.

7) Daniel Linden Duke and Adrienne Maravich
Heckel. Teacher's Guide to Classroom Management.
New York: Random House, 1984. p. 3-4.

8) Robert D. Brumfield and Rex L. Leonard. "The
Student Teaching Experience: A Time to
Consolidate One's Perceptions," College Student
Journal. 17: 401-406. Winter, 1983.

9) Hershel D. Thornburg. Introduction to
Educational Psychology. St. Paul, Minnesota:
West Publishing Co., 1984, p. 438-439.

10) H.D. Thornburg. <u>School Learning and Instruction.</u> Monterey, Ca: Brooks/Cole., 1973.

11) Lee Canter and Marlene Canter. <u>Assertive Discipline.</u> Los Angeles: Canter and Associates, Inc., 1979.

12) C.M. Charles. <u>Elementary Classroom Management.</u> New York: Longman, Inc., 1983., p. 55.

13) Carl H. Rinne. "Low Profile Classroom Controls," <u>Phi Delta Kappan.</u> Sept., 1982. v. 64 n.1. p. 52-55.

14) Vincent R. Rogers. "Laughing with Children," <u>Educational Leadership.</u> April, 1984. v. 41 n. 7. p. 46-49.

15) Lya Krema and Chaya Kurtz. "Locus of Control, Perceptions, and Attributions of Student Teachers in Educational Situations," <u>College Student Journal.</u> 17:245-251. Fall, 1983.

Orienting Inquiry:

1. How do you help a student teacher to meet needs for students at various levels of abilities and interests?

2. How do you help him to prepare for the "average" students?

3. What should you do to prepare and demonstrate creative and individualized instructional activities?

> "The treasure which you think
> not worth taking the trouble and
> pains to find, this one alone
> is the real treasure you are
> longing for all your life."
>   Treasure of the Sierra Madre(1)

This chapter is included in response to a list of needs and inadequacies expressed by student teachers. We hope that you will take some time with your student teacher to show him how you attempt to meet individual needs within a busy schedule. Explain methods that you use to create special activities, to modify the pace of procedure, to change teaching style, to organize challenging research projects for students, or to structure written assignments so that they allow for varying student interests and abilities.

It is a difficult and challenging task for a cooperating teacher to guide the student teacher from large group teaching approaches to individualized and personalized assignments for small groups or individuals. Just learning to teach, choosing appropriate management techniques, organizing curriculum, and attempting to meet broad educational goals are by themselves overwhelming tasks. A concentrated effort to do each task can prevent one from considering and teaching for the individual cognitive and affective needs of students. Many educators feel that student teachers seldom attain individualized instructional approaches during their student teaching. Johnson, Cox, and Wood go farther by stating that pupil learning is seldom the central concern in student teaching. (2)

Student teachers themselves perceive inadequacies in providing for individual student needs. Lane and Morrow noted that the second highest student teacher concern (following "discipline") was the ability to "meet individual differences with appropriate teaching skills." (3) Purcell and Seiferth also discovered that student teachers list the lack of time for individual instruction second only to the ability to manage student behavior. (4)

It is all but impossible for an experienced teacher to approach a total class of students in a way that will promote maximal learning for each one. Student teachers, therefore, must understand that they are not "miracle workers." However, encourage them to try to reach all students by first learning each person's abilities, and then by setting high, but achievable goals for each. It is possible that student teachers, because of their lack of knowledge about some of your "slow" learners, might elicit higher achievement from students whom they encourage and "expect" to accomplish goals that you may have thought were too unrealistic. The self-fulfilling prophecy theory that they learned in their education classes can be practiced as they lead students toward maximizing potentials.

The Average Student

With the recent emphasis on special education and developing opportunities for mainstreaming, some parents express concern that the average students' needs may be neglected. Average students, whose range of interests and abilities are astounding, require as much or more planning and preparing of challenging activities as those who possess exceptional characteristics. Within the wide range of "averageness," some students may require alternative teaching techniques and accommodations to their individual styles of learning. It is a common mistake made by beginning teachers to search for one magical "best" way to reach all students. There is no such magic because each student, average or special, is unique. Some students learn best through games, role playing, and activity-oriented tasks, while others will do best with passive experiences, lectures, readings, or listening to your explanations. Teaching styles must vary, therefore, to meet this spectrum of needs.

Gartner and Riessman (5) explain that individualization requires tremendous effort from teachers. They list six important teacher variables that affect the establishment of individualized learning situations:

1) The personality and attitudes of the teacher affect student learning efforts. An outgoing teacher may be able to reach the "most" students, an empathetic teacher may be able to help students with special worries or needs, an egotistical teacher may be too concerned with his own problems to recognize or consider those of others, etc.

2) Teachers who use one preferred teaching style may reach only certain percentages of their students' needs, whereas teachers who adapt teaching styles to fit the learners reach a greater number.

3) The teacher's ability and willingness to learn, risk, change, and grow influence the need to individualize instruction. Teachers who are flexible and produce a non-threatening atmosphere are the most effective.

4) If a teacher is aware of his own learning style, he may recognize that others learn differently. Learning styles vary from the active, participatory roles to the passive, absorbing roles. Each teacher must be attuned to these differences and prepare to teach in the ways which complement the wide range of learning styles.

5) If a teacher is willing to evaluate his personal teaching style, techniques, and methods, he will be more effective with different kinds of learners. The student teacher should be encouraged to analyze why certain children fail to meet learning objectives. Perhaps success can be achieved through changes in teaching methodology.

6) If you can become a co-learner with students, you can facilitate individual growth. Teachers who admit mistakes and learn with their students are more respected and do achieve better results.

If your student teacher knows the characteristics needed for individualizing teaching, he can evaluate his own learning and teaching preferences. He will be prepared much better to teach for all abilities and extremes within the "average range."

Exceptional Children

All children are exceptional! However, for clarity in this chapter the following definition of exceptional learners will be used. They differ significantly from the average child in any of the following ways: 1) mental characteristics, 2) sensory abilities, 3) physical or neuromuscular characteristics, 4) social or emotional behaviors, 5) communication abilities, or perhaps even 6) multiple handicaps. (6). Expect that about one child in five will exhibit differences in one or more of these categories.

With the introduction of the 1975 Public Law 94-142, equal educational opportunities were mandated for all children in the public schools. Equal opportunity meant legally that all children were to be placed in the "least restrictive learning environment."

Changes have, of course been made in student placements. However, exceptional children are treated differently from school to school and from teacher to teacher. If teachers respect the legal and moral rationales of the I.E.P. (an individual education plan for each student required in P.L. 94-142), they can more effectively meet the students' needs and offer an individualized education in the mainstream of group education.

Student teachers will need help if they are to prepare for the variety of student exceptionalities found in every school population. Although the "labeling" of students should be avoided as much as possible, the following categories (labels) are presented, not as an all inclusive guide, but to help the student teacher toward meeting the unique needs of students who wear these general labels. Each type of exceptionality requires special teaching strategies. Suggestions in the general categories of "handicapped," "culturally different," and "gifted and talented" are presented for guiding the student teacher toward an appropriate understanding. Further readings in special education from the "Chapter 12: Notes" are suggested.

1. Handicapped Students

A handicapped child is any individual who has a functional impairment that precludes normal performance in a specific area. Handicaps usually are categorized as mental, sensory, physical, communication, or learning impairments.

It may be helpful for the student teacher to know that nearly one in eight school age children has one or more of these handicaps. (7)

Many handicapped students require only minor modifications of instructional approaches, such as extended time allotments, more individual directions, or adjustments in the difficulty level of the content. The following guidelines are presented to help you and your student teacher plan and prepare to meet the needs of various handicapped students. Ask your student teacher to:

1. observe and identify any noticeably handicapped children and to cite data and reasons for all judgments.

2. record and describe instructional approaches that you use that are unique for a particular student.

3. discuss the handicapped person's interaction patterns with other students (in both academic and recreational settings).

4. design an I.E.P. for a specific student and be prepared to discuss it in a conference session.

5. plan and teach a lesson that will be assessed on how well the needs of the special students in the class were met.

1. Culturally Different Students

In most classrooms there will be individuals from different cultures and students with beliefs that may be different from yours or your student teacher's. While all students may share many similarities, some also may generate measurable, observable, and important differences from the majority of students.

Many of these differences, such as cognitive skills, nonverbal communication, attitudes, and personalities are known to have impact on the school curriculum. (8) Cultural differences

200

also can influence the way in which students learn and the methods in which the teacher and other students respond. Student teachers should attempt to individualize the curriculum to meet known cultural differences. In addition, they should learn how to use cultural differences to strengthen student acceptance and understanding of culture.

Alessia and Owen, in a handbook for student teachers, present 8 questions to help student teachers become acquainted with how a school provides for needs of culturally different students. You may wish to have your student teacher search for answers to these questions to help him to prepare for these students.

1. From the teachers you have met or seen, does the staff appear to be culturally diverse? administrators? counselors?

2. From what you have observed, do you see any special curricular activities designed to enhance a student's awareness of cultural diversity?

3. Is there evidence of school assemblies, decorations, speakers, holidays, and heroes which reflect ethnic group differences?

4. Do school libraries and resource centers have a variety of materials on the histories, experiences, and culture of different ethnic groups?

5. Are there pictures of minority groups displayed in the room? within the selected texts?

6. Can you detect through observation the economic range of students in the class? If yes, what clues helped you to determine the diversity?

7. Can you identify the racial composition of the classroom? If yes, cite what cultures you have observed and how you determined the diversity.

8. Are you able to recognize the cultural, social, and value diversity among the ethnic groups in the class? Does this recognition help you to plan activities which accommodate this diversity? (9)

You may find that student teachers have limited college course preparation for relating to culturally different students. With the increase of non-English speaking students the task of relating becomes more difficult. You may need to assume a large part of the responsibility in helping the student teacher to adjust, to be tolerant of differences, and to educate these students in the most appropriate and effective methods.

3. Gifted and Talented Children

Gifted and talented students are defined as "the upper 3 to 5 percent of school age children and youth who show outstanding promise in general intellectual ability, specific academic aptitude, creative or productive thinking, psychomotor ability, leadership, and achievement in the visual and performing arts. This definition reflects the trend away from the historical idea of giftedness as simply the ability to achieve high scores on an intelligence test." (10) Many statewide gifted programs, however, continue to accept the more narrow achievement/I.Q. score approach to identify students for special programs. Sometimes leadership, talent, psychomotor skills, and performing arts skills are not even considered when students are selected for gifted programs.

Your student teacher will have the opportunity to see how the gifted and talented students interact in a classroom setting. Because these students are capable of higher than average performance and achievement, they often are not challenged in school. They can become bored and perhaps even become behavior problems. Researchers have indicated that teachers not prepared to recognize or promote exceptional skills and talents sometimes are insensitive and even hostile toward students who do things before instruction or do them in a different way. (11)

Plan together and help your student teacher prepare challenging and worthwhile projects or extensions for these special students. The student teacher also will need guidance to evaluate variations in performance that result from different assignments and individual or special tests. (12) With support and instruction student teachers can understand and prepare for the needs of gifted students. The following five suggestions are presented to guide the student teacher in his preparation for these special gifted and talented students.

Ask the student teacher to:

1. identify the students he perceives to be "gifted," and the characteristics that are demonstrated.

2. examine and critique your techniques for handling these students.

3. design and use questioning techniques and strategies that facilitate higher levels of cognitive and affective development.

4. include additional "challenge" projects in his plans for these students.

5. develop a plan to include these students in creative leadership roles as aids in the daily teaching.

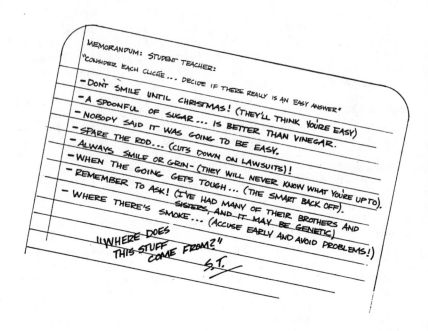

MEMORANDUM: STUDENT TEACHER:
"CONSIDER EACH CLICHE ... DECIDE IF THERE REALLY IS AN EASY ANSWER"

- DON'T SMILE UNTIL CHRISTMAS! (THEY'LL THINK YOU'RE EASY)
- A SPOONFUL OF SUGAR ... IS BETTER THAN VINEGAR.
- NOBODY SAID IT WAS GOING TO BE EASY.
- SPARE THE ROD... (CUTS DOWN ON LAWSUITS)!
- ALWAYS SMILE OR GRIN - (THEY WILL NEVER KNOW WHAT YOU'RE UP TO).
- WHEN THE GOING GETS TOUGH ... (THE SMART BACK OFF).
- REMEMBER TO ASK! (I'VE HAD MANY OF THEIR BROTHERS AND SISTERS, AND IT MAY BE GENETIC)
- WHERE THERE'S SMOKE ... (ACCUSE EARLY AND AVOID PROBLEMS!)

"WHERE DOES THIS STUFF COME FROM?"

S.T.

The Challenge

Teachers have varying opinions of the mainstreaming concept and its effect on students. As Bogdan concludes, it is irrelevant whether mainstreaming is good or bad at this point. The issue is to prepare adequately to meet student needs. (13) Accommodating and enriching individual needs in the same classroom is difficult and challenging for the best of experienced teachers. You, as a cooperating teacher, are in a unique position to help the student teacher learn how to offer both average and exceptional students the best possible experience in the "least restrictive environment." You are the role model that your student teacher requires to "see" how to accomplish these difficult tasks. Your enthusiasm and creativity in meeting this challenge may be one of the best opportunities to promote education.

PROBLEM ANALYSIS No. 50: HANDLING FAVORITISM

Fran has spent four weeks in your classroom. After her introductions, she learned the students' names quickly and researched their backgrounds through the school records. Fran now seems to seek out and identify with a small group of students who have a similar socioeconomic lifestyle. She directs most of her time to these students and is reluctant to work with the students who are not as affluent. These "left out" students are beginning to pick up on her behavior and want to know why she doesn't help them.

MAKING DECISIONS:

As her cooperating teacher, what steps should you take to encourage Fran to be fair to all students despite her inability to "identify" with all classes of students? Should you involve any other persons in a discussion of this problem?

PROBLEM ANALYSIS No. 51: UNPROFESSIONAL CONDUCT

Stephanie has many friends on the middle school faculty. She uses her breaks to talk with them and to get their advice. They apparently have warned her about the students in your class who are "hyperactive," "lazy," "trouble makers," and "dumb." You feel that most of these labels are inaccurate, personally damaging, and

unprofessional. This anger peaks as you hear
Stephanie, in the presence of the whole class,
say "And I'm not the only teacher in the school
that thinks you're lazy!"

MAKING DECISIONS:

After your anger is under control, how would
you proceed with this situation? What position
will you take with the faculty members who label
students? What should you ask of Stephanie to
rectify her actions?

PROBLEM ANALYSIS No. 52: "WRITE I.E.P.'s THAT GUARANTEE SUCCESS"

Your student teacher for your learning
disablities class tells you that she has been
warned not to set goals or list objectives on the
I.E.P. that students may not perform adequately,
or because of their disability, may not
achieve consistently. The reason she gives for
this caution is to protect herself from any legal
accountability due to failure in achievement of
objectives in the I.E.P. She claims that it must
be better to write plans and choose concepts that
you are certain you can teach for mastery.

MAKING DECISIONS:

How do you respond to the position she
chooses for the I.E.P. writing and the teaching
of learning disabled children?

PROBLEM ANALYSIS No. 53: "THE END OF A SPECIAL RELATIONSHIP"

You have an extremely withdrawn child in your special education class. You have tried several techniques to get him to open up, but nothing has worked. Ed, your student teacher, has become close to this student during his first three weeks with you. Showing great patience and several shaping approaches, he has made remarkable progress with the student. In fact, toward the end of Ed's student teaching period, he is able to get the child to participate in several group activities. You now have a dilemma because the child still will not relate to you and Ed will be leaving in a few days.

MAKING DECISIONS:

Do you concede defeat and go on as before? Do you ask Ed to visit occasionally? How will you bridge the gap with the child when Ed leaves? What do you do when you can't always get what's "best for the child?"

PROBLEM ANALYSIS No. 54: "I CAN'T STAND HAVING TO WORK WITH THE HANDICAPPED!"

Scott, your new student teacher, has observed your art classes for several days at the beginning of his experience. He is amazed at the creative abilities of two students, one handicapped with a hearing impairment and the other blind. He admires your patience and the special attention you offer these children. He admits, however, that he never will want to work with handicapped children because he can't overcome his aversion to the association with "people who are not normal." Scott has decided that he only will accept a position to teach in an art school for identified talented children.

MAKING DECISIONS:

How do react to Scott's aversion? Would you force him to get to know the handicapped students and do special art projects with them while he is under your supervision? Does your responsibility extend to changing basic and personal attitudes? Would you mention to him that his so-called "talented art school children" also could include handicapped but talented chilen?

PROBLEM ANALYSIS No. 55: GIFTED KIDS MEET THEIR MATCH!

Gretchen is a very organized and structured student teacher, but generally is uncreative in her approach to student teaching. You have explained that she will need to provide extra activities for the advanced students who finish their assignments early. She designs her plans to include your suggestions.

The following day Gretchen hands these "quick finishers" another assignment--more work of the same they just finished. The students appear to be disappointed, but do the extra assignments. After two more days of this approach, Gretchen notices that all of the students seem to be finishing their seat work at the very same time. She comments that "the quick finishers are now being challenged and are no longer a problem."

MAKING DECISIONS:

How do you proceed with Gretchen? What should you tell her about "more of the same" assignments for talented students? Is one assignment for the total class an example of the self-fulfilling prophecy?

---

1.   For any single content topic in a given class, determine the number of instructional approaches, the level of presentation, the variations of projects and activities, the extensions for further study, and the kinds of remedial activities that you would have to prepare to individualize the instruction for each student or group of very similar students.

2.   Some educators predict the I.E.P. will one day replace the broad spectrum grade level curricular plans currently used in our public schools. If this happens what changes would you suggest for the teacher training institutions, especially for the student teaching experience?

3.   Develop a list of tasks or data collecting activities that would help the student teacher realize the wide variation of abilities and interests that exist in a "normal" class. One example might include examining the range of reading abilities within the class.

1)   Regina   S.   Jones   and   Laurel   N.   Tanner.
"Classroom   Discipline: The   Unclaimed   Legacy,"
Phi Delta Kappan March,   1981   v.62   n.7,   p.   494-
497.

2)   William Johnson, C. Benjamin Cox, and George
Wood.   "Communication   Patterns   and   Topics   of
Single and Paired Student Teachers,"   Action   in
Teacher Eduation. v.   4 n.1, 56-60. Spring/summer
1982.

3)   John   M.   Lane   and   John   E.   Morrow.
"Instructional   Problems   of   Student   Teachers:
Perceptions   of   Student   Teachers,   Supervising
Teachers, and College Supervisors," Action in
Teacher Education. v. 5 n. 1-2. Spring/summer
1983.

4)   Thomas   D. Purcell and Berniece B.   Seiferth.
"Tri-State Survey   of   Student Teachers," College
Student Journal. 16:27-29. Spring, 1982.

5)   Alan   Gartner   and   Frank   Riessman.   How   to
Individualize Learning.   Fastback 100.   Phi Delta
Kappa   Educational   Foundation.   Bloomington,
Indiana, 1977, p. 24.

6)   S.A.   Kirk.   Educating Exceptional Children.
Boston: Houghton Mifflin, 1972.

7)   Hershel   D.   Thornburg.   Introduction   to
Educational Psychology. St.   Paul, Minnesota:
West Publishing Co., 1984.

8)   George E. Uhlig and Alma G. Vasquez. "Cross-
cultural Research   and   Multicultural Education:
1970-1980," Journal of Teacher Education. v. 33
n. 4. July/Aug. 1982, 45-48.

9)   Mary   Alessia   and Kathleen Owens.   Handbook
for   the   Student   Teaching Semester.   Lewis
University, Romesville, Illinois, Sept., 1983.

10) Marsha M. Correll. Teaching the Gifted and Talented. Fastback 119. Phi Delta Kappa Educational Foundation. Bloomington, Ind., 1978, p. 12.

11) Correll, Ibid., p. 36.

12) Patricia Alexander. "Gifted Education: Needed Theory," The Educational Forum. v. XLVIII n. 3 Spring, 1984, p. 285-293.

13) Robert Bogdan. "A Closer Look at Mainstreaming," The Educational Forum. v. XLVII n. 4. Summer, 1983. 425-434.

Orienting Inquiry:

---

1. What should I know about school law if I supervise student teachers?

2. Is there a legal base that establishes "quality" for the practicing cooperating teacher?

3. What is due process?

4. What legal rights are granted to student teachers?

5. To evaluate professional efforts, what legal steps should I observe to protect the student teacher, the school, and myself?

6. How do I reduce the chance of a law suit over due process, negligence, or equal opportunity confrontations?

7. Is it acceptable for my student teacher to assume full responsibility (as a substitute teacher) if I am unable to attend school? Can he "fill in" for another teacher if substitutes are difficult to acquire?

> "The significant legal problems germane to student teaching are the same ones affecting the profession at large." (1)

As a cooperating teacher you especially must be cognizant of those public school laws which affect the profession at large as well as those specific laws of your state. First of all, you are responsible for the welfare and safety of the students in your class. There are specific legal ramifications added when you accept a student teacher. Essentially you cannot reassign your legal responsibility for the students to your student teacher. The student teacher should be acquainted with basic public school law, but you need to instruct him about specific legal protections which cover children, faculty, and school district personnel. In this chapter we will explore the legal relationship that exists between you and your student teacher, the importance of due process, and the types of legal suits that have resulted from student teacher/supervisor/school relationships.

Each state varies regarding laws and regulations that cover supervisory and student teacher expectations. However, the general considerations presented in this chapter will provide you with adequate background and basic information. You also should review your own state laws to clarify points that may be unusual or very specific in your state.

Statutory Authority and Student Teaching

A statute is an act of a legislature in certain form such that it becomes the law governing conduct within its domain. All fifty states have some statutory provisions for teacher education. The question which is immediate to your concern may be, "Does my state have statutes authorizing or governing the act of student teaching in our schools?" Morris and Curtis reported that forty states provide statutory authority for student teaching. Four states (Alabama, Massachusetts, Maine, and New Hampshire) anticipate providing a statute for student teaching and six states (Georgia, Hawaii, Rhode Island, Vermont, Virginia, and Wisconsin) neither have nor were anticipating a provision for such statutory authority. (2) This number of forty is a tremendous increase from 1966 when Swalls reported that only six states had provided statutory authority for student teaching. (3) The lack of state statutes for student teaching in the above mentioned states does not mean that there are problems with getting student teachers into the school systems. These states merely have chosen not to designate specific laws for student teaching.

215

Legal Base for "Quality" Cooperating Teachers

"Even though field-based experiences have been recognized as one of the most important components of teacher preparation programs, very little has been done to provide legal support systems which would assure reasonable, qualitative standards. States, primarily through program standards and by legislative mandate, have moved to require early field experiences and extensions of student teaching without provisions for adequate support necessary to insure qualitative experiences." (4)

Some states are working on legislation to guarantee quality-based student teaching experiences. For example, Georgia provides programs which lead to the endorsement of certification in the supervision of student teaching. Texas requires cooperatively developed inservice improvement programs for supervisory teachers. (5) However, Haberman and Harris reported that 24 out of 50 states have no written legal requirements. Of the 26 states that have some type of mandates for cooperating teachers, 16 require two or three years of teaching experience before accepting a student teacher, nine require a program or course in the supervision of student teachers, three mandate a masters degree in education, and two require that a teacher be certified. (6)

As the need for better trained teachers intensifies, states will move, through legal actions, to improve the quality of the teacher preparation programs. Most states support the belief that the student teaching experience is essential to becoming a good teacher. We feel, therefore, that legal provisions eventually will be made to cover the training and selecting efforts of the cooperating teachers. In nearly every area improved coursework, required classes, masters degree completion, inservice training, and supervisory certification programs are coming under closer inspection with major changes expected. Legal provisions will accompany most changes.

Understanding Due Process

In North Carolina in 1973 (Moore v. Gaston County Board of Education) a student teacher was discharged from student teaching because of his stated approval of Darwinian theory and his open questioning of the literal interpretation of the Bible in the classroom. However, the Fourteenth Amendment and the North Carolina Statutes of Protection which assure due process of law, were violated when he was discharged by the Board without appropriate procedures. After a court review, he was allowed to continue his student teaching. (7)

This case illustrates the necessity for teachers and administrators to understand the significance of due process in the public school setting, especially for the student teaching experience. Due process of law is a phrase which was first introduced in the Fifth Amendment to the Constitution. The phrase was made applicable to the states with the adoption of the Fourteenth Amendment, Section 1, which states that "Nor shall any State deprive any person of life, liberty, or property, without due process of law." Due process of law does not have a fixed meaning. It adjusts with changing jurisprudential values. Procedural due process is concerned with the method or procedure by which decisions are made. Its basic element is fairness, and it requires adequate notice and the right to a fair hearing before any actions are taken. (8) Courts have required, in the procedural due process issue, that actions of any school officials or board members not be arbitrary, discriminatory, or unreasonable. Substantive due process identifies those constitutional rights which school authorities may not penalize or limit without substantial justification.

A 1979 case illustrates the importance of using due process correctly. The case involved John Aubuchon, a student teacher who deviated from his lesson plans, had difficulty in

217

accepting criticism, failed to detect and correct grammatical errors, had a tendency to overidentify with students, and exhibited other inappropriate behaviors. A meeting was arranged to include the student teacher, university supervisor, cooperating teacher, and assistant high school principal to discuss and try to resolve the problems. However, during the meeting, the student teacher was uncooperative and did not respond to the questions being raised. Aubuchon was ordered out of the school by the assistant principal. The University supervisor wrote a letter to the Associate Dean of Education expressing Aubuchon's "strange behavior" and his possible "need of psychological help." After reviewing the deficiencies outlined in the letter, the Associate Dean requested that Aubuchon withdraw voluntarily from student teaching. Twelve days later, Aubuchon, who had not withdrawn, received a letter advising him that he had been dropped administratively from the course. Aubuchon sued, alleging that his due process rights were being violated and that decisions were arbitrary and that the note written about him would impose a stigma to his reputation. The court ruled against the student teacher, stating that his due process rights were not violated. There is no requirement for a hearing when a student is being dismissed for academic deficiencies. The court also concluded that the decision made by the dean to drop the student from the course was made in good faith, not arbitrarily. (9)

This case is enough of a warning to alert administrators to the need to understand and practice due process. It is advisable, in ensuring due process, that steps be formal with written or recorded information and with all involved parties present. Helm emphasizes that to assure required due process, supervisors of clinical experiences "should conduct their supervision and write their evaluations with a concern for: factual and objective statements; early, specific, and written notice to students having problems; communication of a student's weaknesses only to those who need to know; and avoidance of malicious or intentionally harmful behavior. While most supervisors probably

operate according to these guidelines already,
the occurrence of that occasional, unsatisfactory
performance requires ready familiarity with the
precautions available to a supervisor who wants
to stay out of court." (10)

In the student teaching situation, it is
important for you, the cooperating teacher, to be
aware of and to use several procedures necessary
to ensure due process. The following statements
by Long (who summarized a report by Olson, Moody,
and McGrath) include fifteen suggestions to help
cooperating teachers with due process.

Assuring Due Process as a Cooperating Teacher

A. Student teachers must be provided with a specific and complete statement of public school requirements and expectations.

B. The student teacher must be provided with a specific description of the competencies by which he or she will be evaluated, detailing the processes to be employed.

C. Actual supervisor practice at both the school and college level must be consistent with published policy available to the student teacher in advance.

D. In an early orientation student teachers should be given, in writing, both the supervisor and institutional requirements.

E. Supervisory observations should be frequent, comprehensive, recorded, and followed up.

F. Conferences should be held after observations and should include a detailed written summary, with copies retained by student and supervisor.

G. Adequate conferring time must be provided throughout the program.

H. Evaluation must be within the context of improvement of stated competencies.

I. Grades awarded must relate directly to the stated criteria for those grades.

J. Supervisors should maintain continual, factual, objective, and written records on each student teacher they supervise, and the student teacher should receive a copy.

K. Students should be informed in advance of the steps that will ensure due process for them.

L. It should be made clear that clinical experiences are courses taken within the curricular framework of the university and that academic policy governs them, not student disciplinary policy or any other policy outside that framework. Removal from student teaching does not require a full hearing if it is for academic reasons.

M. Every effort should be made to let students participate in decisions made about them and to know the data upon which those decisions were made.

N. Students may continue in the clinical experience as long as they complete established requirements and demonstrate at least the stated minimum levels of competence.

O. Students teachers may be removed from the clinical experience if it is determined that the students or youth are suffering from their presence, or if it is determined that they would have a better experience with another placement. (11)

This list can serve as a guide to proper legal practices. It is included as a checklist for cooperating teachers and administrators to review periodically. With society becoming increasingly litigious, you must be aware of the implications for ensuring due process. It is no fun going to court to defend against sloppy procedure. It may take more time and effort to comply with procedure and paper work, but you must provide frequent written assessments and confer often and openly with a student teacher. He must be informed of progress and aware of his strengths and weaknesses. These two steps will eliminate most of the legal difficulties that supervisors encounter.

Court Cases Dealing with Student Teachers

Cooperating teachers may feel some comfort in the fact that there have been relatively few court cases relating to student teachers. Swalls, in his research of law and student teaching, found that between 1906-1975 there were only fourteen court cases. He classified these cases into four major categories:

221

1. Legal authority to permit student teaching in public schools.
2. Tort liability of student teachers. (causing injury to another through violation of some legal duty)
3. Certification and welfare of student teachers.
4. Legal authority for acceptance, assignment, and dismissal of student teachers.

An example of tort liability can be found in the case Garner v. State of New York. In this case a student teacher was found negligent for an injury resulting to a pupil who tried unsuccessfully to do a head stand in a physical education class. (12)

In two cases the courts upheld colleges' denial for student teaching placements. Both cases involved the moral character of the student teachers. In Lai v. Board of Trustees of East Carolina University (1971), a student teacher was denied application for his student teaching assignment. The student teacher had been arrested for possession of dangerous drugs, but these charges were dropped. However, the student teacher did admit to smoking marijuana. The court ruled that university officials are entitled to wide discretion in the training of their students and ruled for the institution.

In James v. West Virginia Board of Regents (1971), a student teacher was denied the right to student teach because of his reputation as a militant. The college officials contacted several counties to request placement for him, but they declined on the basis of his reputation and his violent disturbances at the college. Again the court dismissed the suit against the college and allowed the evidence of general reputation as admissible and an exception to the "heresay rule." (13)

A 1981 national study of student teacher programs by Johnson and Yates identified 48 lawsuits recently settled or in various stages of litigation. Concerns regarding provision of due process are evident in at least 26 of these cases. (14) Although the law suits are increasing in student teaching situations, apart from the usual risk of suits for negligence, the law at this point speaks rather gently to both student teachers and supervisors.

The Legal Rights of Student Teachers

Many states have legal provisions which grant that student teachers have the same rights as teachers. These rights are guaranteed specifically. For example, in North Carolina State law, it states that "a student teacher under the supervision of a certified teacher or principal shall have the protection of the law accorded the certified teacher." (15) Nebraska law states that "a student teacher or intern under the supervision of a certified teacher, principal, or other administrator shall have the protection of the laws accorded the certified teacher, principal, or other administrator. (16) In many other states these provisions are unwritten, but "assumed."

The issue of regulating pupil conduct is a concern for most student teachers. Although many states have legal provisions that imply that student teachers have authority to regulate pupil conduct, only six states have expressed this authority in a statute. (Illinois, Indiana, Nebraska, North Carolina, North Dakota and West Virginia). (17)

States also have been moving toward the inclusion of liability of student teachers for injuries to pupils in accidents. Four states (Connecticut, Iowa, New Jersey, and New York) provide a mandatory "safe-harmless provision" and ten states (Colorado, Illinois, Maryland, North Dakota, Utah, Idaho, Indiana, Minnesota, Ohio, and Wyoming) have authorized provisions for liability insurance to cover student teachers. (18) Several other states are developing similar legislation.

A case that exemplifies the move toward treating student teachers as employees in terms of liability occurred in 1979 when Donald Dittmar, a student teacher, was injured while supervising fifth grade students on a school playground. The Court ruled that since he was performing the duties of a student teacher at the time of his injury, he was "placed" within the meaning of the statute and therefore could be entitled to workman's compensation. (19) It is important to realize, however, that such statutes do differ from state to state.

Use of the student teacher as a substitute teacher produces another legal issue concerning the duties and rights of student teachers. The law applies if the student teacher is the substitute for a day when the cooperating teacher is absent or if he fills in for another teacher for a day. The best advice offered in this area is "don't!" Rights and responsibilities as a substitute teacher are ambiguous in most state statutes. There are a few states such as Kansas that express a specific position. ("Certified student teachers are prohibited from serving as regular or substitute teachers in Kansas schools while performing student teaching.") (20) Because of potential legal implications and lack of clarity about the issue, it is not recommended to use a student teacher as a substitute teacher.

The Law and Unacceptable Performance

It is best to know the legal steps that must be used to avoid professional liability in cases where the student teacher must be removed from the classroom for unacceptable performance. "The evaluation of the rare student whose teaching has been unacceptable, if not a disaster, is written with the trepidation that accomplishes such concerns as 'what if John decides to challenge my assessment of his performance? Or worse yet, what if he decides to sue me for ruining his career? Could I be charged with libel?'" (21)

A cooperating teacher who writes negative evaluations must protect himself against potential libel charges. Libel is defined as a written form of defamation generally including false or intentional communication that places another person in a position of disgrace, ridicule, or contempt. (22) Helm offers five statements of advice that minimize the chances that your actions could promote a charge of libel:

1) include only statements of fact rather than opinion, and objective rather than subjective descriptions of the student's behavior.

2) limit the information to that which is relevant to or affects the student's performance in the classroom and school.

3) avoid public statements about the student's deficiencies.

4) avoid any personal behavior or statements suggesting malice or intent to harm.

5) convey, by behavior and in writing if possible, a concern both for the student's welfare and the school's welfare, limiting the likelihood of "bad faith or ill will" charges. (23)

Follow an appropriate sequence of due process procedures to deal with an unsatisfactory student teacher. After frequent observations and conferences which list the problems and the statements of expected changes, you should notify in writing the student teacher, the principal, and the college supervisor. These actions should be performed by the middle of the student teaching experience. The student teacher must be instructed in what things he can do to improve his performance. Again, frequent observation techniques should be used and conferences with adequate discussions should occur. To know that if the student teacher is "not improving" or that his actions may be "detrimental to the pupils" can be the basis for removal. Either the college supervisor or the cooperating teacher may ask for removal of a student teacher. The key to adequate supervision is appropriate and written documentation of all issues presented openly with all concerned parties.

Laws are established and enforced to protect individual rights and property. You, your students and parents, and your student teacher should enjoy these guarantees so that teachers can learn to practice and promote education in a safe, socially acceptable, and instructional environment. The rules are simple, but to neglect a basic respect for the procedures tempts disaster.

PROBLEM ANALYSIS No. 56: MORE THAN YOU WANT TO HEAR

William is an effective student teacher. He relates well to students and faculty. Your concern is your legal responsibility and/or conscience when he confides in you that he manages the stress from tough teaching days by using several kinds of drugs. He says that they help him to relax and be prepared for the next day. You have not as yet noticed unusual behavior in the classroom and would not have suspected William to be using drugs of any kind.

MAKING DECISIONS:

Why is William telling you about his use of drugs? Should you be a "narc" and relate his drug use (as he tells you) to the college supervisor? Is it a violation of school policy? How would you proceed?

PROBLEM ANALYSIS No. 57: MAKING QUICK JUDGMENTS

Your student teacher has a pupil that declines to participate in recess or physical education class. The student teacher notices that the non-participant's shirt is stained and seem to stick to his back. He moves the student to the bleachers and asks him what is wrong with his back. The student begins to cry and pulls up his shirt to reveal several welts made with a belt-like instrument. The injuries are bleeding and appear to be infected.

Your student teacher, certain that this a child abuse case, leaves the group of students in the gym to find you in the classroom. He demands that you call the authorities immediately or he will.

MAKING DECISIONS:

What comments can you make about the student teacher's approach? What should you tell him about leaving the class unattended? Step by step, what is the best way to handle this total situation?

PROBLEM ANALYSIS NO. 58: IS MY STUDENT TEACHER A THIEF?"

Marybeth is a very cooperative person. She has completed all assignments and has done a splendid job with the students. She and the children have had a wonderful time together and significant cognitive gains have been made.

During the period of her student teaching, however, some items have disappeared such as your pocket calculator, your digital stop watch, and $22.06 in book money. Marybeth is known to enter the building as early as 7:00 to prepare for the day and to stay as late as 4:30. Early one morning you saw her coming from another room from which some money was missing. There had been no similar problems at this school before her student teaching began. She has only one week until she completes her experience with you.

MAKING DECISIONS:

Would you confront Marybeth, do nothing and hope that there will be an end to the missing items, or go immediately to her college supervisor for advise? Suggest another approach you might try before doing any of the above actions.

PROBLEM ANALYSIS NO. 59:   WHO IS AT FAULT?

Jim is very creative and uses new and unusual teaching methods that are so successful that you plan to use them at a later time. He has excellent control of the class and therefore you feel comfortable leaving the room more frequently during the past two weeks.

One evening a student and his mother come to your home and show you a large bruise on the student's shoulder. They tell you that Jim has pinched him as well as four other students for misbehavior while you were out of the room. They tell you that he also has physically threatened most of the class members. If this is true, Jim is very much out of line and in deep trouble. However, you also may be in legal trouble for negligence because of your absences during these incidents.

MAKING DECISIONS:

Should you be worried about how to cover for your negligence? Should you take Jim out of the teaching situation until you clear up the complaint? Who else should you involve in this mess? Give a step by step procedure from the time of the complaint until the termination of the problem.

PROBLEM ANALYSIS No. 60: A BID FOR STUDENT
ANARCHY

The students in one of your classes are organizing a "walkout" because of a series of confrontations with your student teacher. In another class, students have presented you with two questions in a petition signed by a large number of individuals. ("Do you think that the student teacher was right in the way she handled Paul?" "What will happen to the students who walk out?")

MAKING DECISIONS:

As the cooperating teacher what steps (if any) would you take to prevent anarchy with the students, with the student teacher, and with the administration and college?

1. Check over your student teacher handbook. Would the requirements, rules and regulations, and procedures stand the legal test if the student teacher should take you to court for being arbitrary, unreasonable, lacking in appropriate procedure, discrimination, or failing to produce adequate notice of dissatisfaction?

2. The principal is hard-pressed for chaperones for the football bus trip and asks the student teacher (for no pay) to show up after school, ride the bus, sit in the student section with the students, return on the bus, and wait with the students until their parents arrive to take them home. List ten potential scenarios that could spell legal trouble for the student teacher, the principal, the school, and the students involved if the student teacher were allowed to assume this sole responsibility.

3. Design a case study in which the student teacher would have to make decisions about students based on the accurate use of due process.

NOTES: CHAPTER 13

1) U. R. Hazard. Student Teaching and the Law. Washington, D.C.:   ERIC Clearinghouse on Teacher Education, 1976.

2)   John E. Morris and K. Fred Curtis.   "Legal Issues Relating to Field-Based Experiences in Teacher   Education," Journal   of   Teacher Education.   v. 34 n. 2. p. 2-6. March/April, 1983.

3)   Fred   Swalls. Legal   Aspects of Student Teaching. Cooperative Research Project S-075. Danville,   Ill.: The Interstate Printers and Publishers, 1966.

4)   Morris and Curtis, Ibid., p. 2-6.

5) John E. Morris, J. Donald Hawk, and Eldon Drake. "Most   Frequently   Used   Methods   and Criteria   for   Identifying,   Selecting,   and Continuing Supervising Teachers," The   Teacher Educator. v. 17 n. 3. Winter 1981/82. p. 14-23.

6)   M.   Haberman   and   P.   Harris. "State Requirements for Cooperating Teachers," Journal of Teacher Education. 1982.   33 (3) 45-47.

7) Fred Swalls. The Law on Student Teaching in the United States. Danville, Ill: Interstate Printers and Publishers, 1976.

8)   Steven H. Gifis. Law Dictionary. New York: Baron's Educational Series, 1975.

9) Virginia Helm. "Defamation, Due Process, and Evaluating Clinical   Experiences," Action   in Teacher Eduation. v. 4 n. 2. Fall, 1982, p. 27-32.

10) Fred Swalls. Ibid. (The Law on Student Teaching).p. 17.

11)   Swalls, Ibid. 20-23.

12)   Swalls, Ibid. 22-23.

13)   Long, _Ibid._ 29-33.

14)   Swalls, _Ibid._ p.58.

15)   North   Carolina   General   Statutes.   Section
115-160.6.

16)   Nebraska   School   Law.   Section   79-1298.
1975.

17)   Swalls, _Ibid._ p.58.

18)   Swalls, _Ibid._ p. 59.

19)   Kansas   Administrative   Regulations.   91-19-
10.

20)   Helm, _Ibid._   p. 27.

21)   M.   McCarthy   and Nelda H. Cambron.   _Public
School Law: Teachers'   and Students' Rights._
Boston: Allyn and Bacon, Inc., 1981., p. 180.

22)   Helm, _Ibid.,_ p. 31.

14 Concluding Perspectives on Supervising A Student Teacher

Orienting Inquiry:

---

1. How does a cooperating teacher determine the extent to which he influences a student teacher?

2. In what ways (both formally and informally) will I be evaluated as a cooperating teacher?

3. How can a cooperating teacher evaluate his own efforts?

₁₀ Teach

Do I dare to teach,
to   use   that   voice   that   sometimes
    hides
behind my face, within my eyes
and speak with force
for love, for joy, for peace?
Can I, should I teach?
Do I dare to lead?

What is wrong and what is right
or is there only in this life
a design
that moves us, each
in different directions
despite our hopes,
choose what we might?
Can I choose or am I pegged
to fit only into a given space,
to stay there,
posing in a certain way?
I wonder, do I dare to teach?

They tell me confidence will grow
but now it's only in
quiet golden moments that I know
that I may go forward
and leap into the rugged sea
that is what it is to teach.
And all we may do is our best. (1)

The success in classroom supervision depends largely on the willingness and ability of those involved to join forces with the total teacher education team to learn from and with each other. Fortunately many teachers, college personnel, and apprentice teachers renew and demonstrate this strong commitment each year. Those supervisors do try to develop accurate observation skills, data collecting methods, logical analytical skills, broad planning techniques, and fair and just evaluation procedures. These expectations and implied competencies often are not reflected in the certification requirements for supervision credentials. It is hoped that the structured and organized procedures suggested in this text will produce measurable results which you can identify as valuable in your role as a cooperating teacher. It is also desired that the credential requirements and supervision courses and training will improve to be more responsive to the needs of the cooperating teacher. It is necessary also to increase the requirements used to screen potential cooperating teachers. Improved screening methods will help to guarantee competence in supervision skills, to assure abilities to work well with others, and to select those serious professionals who want to work with student teachers. (2)

Is it really worth all the effort? Having studied the responsibilities, legal concerns, potential problem student teachers, time commitments, and preparation and skills needed to supervise a student teacher, you may question the energies required compared to the rewards generated. Not every student teacher will produce a feather for your cap. Yet, the field of education needs young, excited, energetic, and dedicated people. To assure that these teachers become these types of leaders, we need successful role models and professional associates--the cooperating teachers. The instrinsic rewards of guiding a motivated, yet inexperienced person to a station of accomplishment, success, and self-esteem are immeasurable.

DiLiberto, a new high school teacher, stated during his senior year in college that "I want to be a teacher! I want to be the best teacher that any child ever listened to, learned from, and loved. I want to be the one to show parents that professionalism is still alive in education. I want to be the one to show future college students that there is success and happiness in education. Most importantly, I want to be the one that is so witty, intelligent, sincere, and unique, that one of my fourth graders has the sudden thought, 'I want to be like him, I want to be a teacher.!'" (3)

Cooperating teachers are influential role models. The cooperating teacher's actions, attitudes, voice inflection, and personality are subject to imitation at all times. The efforts cooperating teachers make toward improving the student teacher's self-concept may be the most important contribution a person can offer to a fellow human. Student teachers with a positive self-image use their perceptions to an advantage with classroom children. Your influence to help the student teacher to feel good about himself has both a multiplying and a lasting effect.

It appears that during the next few years many more cooperating teachers may be asked to utilize their professional skills to help assure the quality and numbers of new teachers needed. Projections from the National Center for Educational Statistics are indicative of the need to produce good student teachers.

Table: Estimated Supply and Demand
for New Teachers in Elementary and
Secondary Schools (in thousands)

Year (fall)	Estimated supply	Estimated demand
1987	187	192
1988	203	189
1989	220	198
1990	238	217

(4)

Vollmer (1984) explains that the number of graduates in teacher education for 1988 will meet only 80.5% of projected need for new teachers. There also is the potential for problems relating to the quality of the candidates entering the field. Some of the problems may be resolved through extended field experiences. (5) Certainly the colleges and universities following the recommendations of the Holmes and Carnegie reports will be demanding a longer time for public school student teaching. It seems therefore, that during the next few years many more cooperating teachers will be required. You may be asked to participate in some of these efforts and therefore will need to consider your philosophical position regarding the supervision question.

"Measuring Up" as a Cooperating Teacher

Evaluation by others and self-evaluation are generally expected for a student teacher. As the cooperating teacher you also should be concerned with evaluating your own efforts and the quality of help you give to the student teacher. Colleges sometimes ask the student teacher to evaluate the performance of the cooperating teacher. It is difficult to assess efforts without specific guidelines and the typical general evaluations usually are not much help in the diagnosis of your own strengths and weaknesses. Therefore several suggestions are included here to help you to obtain more specific data about your effectiveness as a supervisor.

One means of learning about your performance is to require your student teacher to develop an essay at the midway point and at the conclusion of his experience. Using a title such as "Reflections on Teaching," ask him to spell out his philosophy of education, current feelings about education, concerns about working with students, and other insights gained during the student teaching experience. These reflections will provide you with dimensions of your role as a teacher and as a supervisor.

Another measure of your effectiveness and value can be gained by requesting each student teacher, at the end of the student teaching experience to write a letter entitled "From One Student Teacher to Another." The purpose of the letter is to allow the experience of an "old" student teacher to guide the "new" student teacher. As you can see from the following sample letter: 1) several rather important lessons became apparent, 2) there was considerable respect shown for the cooperating teacher, and 3) the writer has rather positive feelings about education and students in general.

Dear Anxious Peer, (From one student teacher to another),

Even though I don't know you, I feel that I should say a few words about the tasks you are about to begin. The key to a successful student teaching experience is you! It is very important that you become acquainted with your cooperating teacher and that you prepare yourself mentally before you ever step into the classroom.

You may be saying, "How do I know exactly what I'll be teaching?" That's why you get acquainted early with your cooperating teacher. Most teachers can tell you what unit or units you will be required to do. You can explain to your teacher what you would like to do, get their ideas and then work hard to make your choices appropriate and applicable. Find out from speaking with your teacher what he or she expects of you and what behavior he expects of his students, including preferred disciplinary styles. Always remember it is still his classroom. Your cooperating teacher can be your greatest resource, so build the relationship as much as you can <u>before</u> you begin to teach.

As I mentioned, mental preparation is a most important point to remember. Great lesson plans and ideas can fail in the classroom if you are not ready mentally. Teaching lessons in front of your peers does not compare to the actual classroom experience. It is imperative that you establish respect and discipline immediately-- it's easier to "let down" than it is to "crack down." Also know the setting of your classroom inside and out, know how much time routine details like role call take. Know how you would react to certain classroom energencies and always be prepared for your students before they arrive-- nothing starts the class period off on the wrong foot worse than if you can't find the role book! Preparation and organization are essential.

Sincerely,

"Glad it's over, but pleased with myself"

In addition you could use the following evaluation checklist to identify activities and duties that are judged to be important enough to be included in the student teaching experience. At the completion of the semester, look over each responsibility and determine your performance as the cooperating teacher. It also may be beneficial to have the student teacher review and rate the value of your efforts in developing his experience and preparation.

Cooperating Teacher Evaluation Checklist

	Self-Eval.	Stud. Teacher Evaluation
1. Demonstrate and explain the major activities of a public school teacher.		
2. Create an atmosphere in which the student teacher can be accepted as a professional colleague.		
3. Promote relationships between the student teacher and students, staff, and community.		
4. Orient student teacher to facilities and equipment.		
5. Lead him to effective teaching through a developmental program paced to his needs and abilities.		
6. Help him develop effectiveness in teaching through joint planing, conferences, and data collection.		
7. Demonstrate and clarify effective teaching strategies.		

241

	Self-Eval.	Stud. Teacher Evaluation
8. Encourage him to develop an individual teaching style.		
9. Clarify teaching assignments and instructional planning procedures.		
10. On a daily basis, provide adequate analysis of student teacher's performance.		
11. Maintain continuity by explaining the total program for the year.		
12. Hold periodic conferences relating to teaching performance.		
13. Survey and approve instructional plans.		
14. Prepare and discuss midterm evaluations.		
15. File appropriate evaluation forms to the college supervisor.		

"NEITHER OF US WILL EVER BE THE SAME."

A Final Note---

     Henry Brooks Adams stated a truism when he said "a teacher affects eternity; he can never tell where his influence stops." If you are interested in effectiveness and "spin off masterpieces," consider the following statistics. A cooperating teacher who supervises three elementary student teachers may be an influence on a potential 750 students over only ten years. A cooperating teacher who guides three secondary education student teachers has a potential influence upon 3,750 middle or high school students during the same ten year period. The cooperating teacher is the most essential element in the production of future teachers. The onus for creating major improvement in the profession will be with the profession itself. (7) The authors feel strongly that our education system can be improved directly and most effectively during the training process for new teachers by the well-qualified, competent, and concerned cooperating teacher. Education needs you, prospective teachers need you, students need you, and society needs you. Welcome to student teacher supervision and good luck as a teacher of teachers!

PROBLEM ANALYSIS No. 61: IS SUPERVISION WORTH THE EFFORT?

You have been supervising student teachers for fourteen years. Your state legislature recently has passed a new regulation that requires all cooperating teachers to complete a three hour masters level workshop on the supervision of student teachers. You never have had a graduate class in supervision, but you feel that you do a good job of working with student teachers.

MAKING DECISIONS:

What would you give up if you decide to relinquish your work with student teachers? What would student teachers lose if you "pull strings" and continue to supervise without the required workshop? Besides satisfying the requirements and perhaps a certificate, what are the other benefits of taking part in such a class or workshop?

Applying Ideas:

In a small group, design a specific evaluation device for the student teacher to complete which rates the effectiveness of the cooperating teacher. Checklists should be included in the Student Teacher Handbook.

NOTES: CHAPTER 14

1. Deborah Elliot. "To Teach," Kappa Delta Pi Record. v. 19 n. 4. Summer, 1983, p. 108.

2. ASCD Yearbook: Supervision of Teaching. Edited by Thomas J. Sergiovanni. Alexandria, Va., p. 183-185.

3. Richard A. Libiberto, Jr. "I Want to Be a Teacher," Kappa Delta Pi Record. Summer, 1984. v. 20 n. 4., p. 113.

4. Projections of Education Statistics to 1990-91, Volume 1: Analytical Report. National Center for Education Statistics.

5. Marian L. Vollmer. "A Case for Extended Clinical Experiences," Action in Teacher Education. v. 6 n. 1-2. Spring/summer, 1984. p. 79-83.

6. W.V.U., Morgantown, W.V., Student Teaching Handbook, 1984.

7. Kenneth Howey, Sam Yarger, and Bruce Joyce. Improving Teacher Education. Palo Alto, CA.: Association of Teacher Educators, 1978.

Note: This type of guide can be prepared by the cooperating teacher or the staff at a particular school to use with student teachers. Because of the changing nature of school life, revisions would be necessary to maintain the effectiveness of the handbook. It is important to note that this sample is merely to provide one type of guide. It is encouraged by the authors to use creative ideas and suggestions which would be more pertinent to your own situation.

List of the staff, faculty members, and traveling teachers

Enrollment list of students

Seating charts and open charts of seating arrangements in which names could be added later

Master schedule of the school day including teacher arrival and dismissal times

Teacher schedules of individual periods

Building floorplan of the classrooms and other areas

Duties of teachers with explanations (bus, cafeteria, lunch, recess, etc.)

Instructions for special emergency drills (fire, bomb threats, tornado, etc.)

Explanation of homeroom period and its components (times, activities allowed, functions to be completed, required procedures such as pledge)

List of textbooks used

List of specific classroom rules (if different from general school policy)

List of school regulations, philosophy, and policy

A guide for writing lesson plans and a sample lesson plan

A guide for designing long range plans and sample long range plan

Expectations of the student teacher (For example, you will:
- arrive at a regular time each day
- be present at established conference sessions
- observe and critique other teachers in the school
- be given a limited time to learn individual student names
- be assigned daily record keeping
- be asked to complete three learning activity bulletin boards
- prepare written lesson plans to be submitted two days prior to instruction
- prepare tests for examination and discussion two days prior to use
- assume responsibility for teaching the entire curriculum by the fourth week
- design and teach a unit plan that incorporates at least three subject areas
- attend professional school meetings
- give notification by 7:00 A.M. if unable to be at school
- be expected to self-evaluate progress and participate in conference sessions
- be willing to try various teaching techniques
- maintain professional demeanor with students and staff
- demonstrate enthusiasm for teaching.)

What you can expect from the cooperating teacher (For example, I will:
- introduce you to the school staff and faculty
- provide an atmosphere of acceptance by students

familiarize you with the classroom,
    school, and available resources
introduce and discuss class routines
    and procedures
provide daily observations of your work
offer immediate feedback
provide opportunities for actual
    teaching experience
be a role model for a variety of
    techniques, approaches, and
    methods
provide an opportunity for you to work
    as a professional colleague
provide continuous evaluation
keep in touch with the college
    supervisor
be available both in school and after
    school
    to give support if problems arise
write the final evaluation report for
    your college and letters of
    recommendation if you request
    them.)

    Desirable attributes of an effective
classroom:

    Students are interested and busy with
productive assignments.
    Evaluation efforts indicate learning
occurred.
    Students are able to work in groups and
independently.
    Students are respective of each other.
    Behavior problems are minimal.
    Exceptional students are given
additional, challenging, or individualized work.
    Questions are asked on all levels of
cognition.
    Materials are organized in a productive
way.
    Various types of teaching occur and
flexibility is obvious.

Sample Daily Observation Checklist

The Lesson:
content objectives
organization
materials
introduction
development
promotion of intellectual skills
closure
The Teacher:
attitude
appearance
poise and confidence
knowledge of content
teaching environment
communication
flexibility
recognition of individual differences
stimulating/motivating

The Students:

behavior
attentiveness and participation
achievement
attitudes

The following suggestions were selected by the authors from a list compiled by Womack (1983) and contain some interesting insight and advice that former student teachers offer for future student teachers. Pass them along to your student teachers and assure them that they are not alone in "worrying just about everything."

Be yourself. The "don't smile 'till January" stuff is for the birds.

Students will want to come into your classroom if you have a smile on your face.

The student teacher should also have very friendly relationships with all the teachers.

Cooperate with others in your school.

Be positive about discipline.

Be prepared to stand up for yourself. Do not let the students rule you.

Let kids know you are human! Laugh at your own mistakes.

Be consistent with your means of discipline. The students do notice if you aren't.

A student teacher should know more about different ways to discipline children without being too severe.

Set up rules and stick to them.

Try to overcome exhaustion if at all possible. Get plenty of rest.

Treat your students as people, not objects. They deserve your respect and you should expect theirs.

Be prepared to spend most of your time at

student teaching. <u>No</u> <u>social</u> <u>life</u> and don't plan a wedding one week afterwards.

When planning lessons you will probably want to overplan at first. If you plan to discuss, write the appropriate questions down. Always have plenty to do in case your students finish early.

Be prepared for things to move along at a fast pace and have enough plans made out to cover this.

Be as organized as you can be. This is the key to most of your work.

Discuss weaknesses you feel you have with your cooperating teacher. She will probably be able to help you strengthen these areas.

If for some reason you are having a bad time, look at yourself before criticizing the students' behavior.

Grow and learn from each experience.

Accept criticism and learn from it. You'll feel better.

Please your university supervisor. Be excited about teaching. (1)

(1) Sid T. Womack, "Suggestions from Student Teachers," ERIC., May, 1983.

Appendix C
Sample Student Teacher Manual

(Note from the authors: This sample handbook has been abstracted from a manual prepared by a high school science and chemistry teacher, Mrs. Nancy Martin. It is included in this text as an example of what a cooperating teacher should prepare for a student teacher. Please realize that every manual will be quite different in content and organization because of major differences in geographic locations, content areas, student ages, and philosophies of education. This sample is only a guideline for what might be included in your manual. Be creative, flexible, and as helpful to your student teachers as you can in the preparation of this handbook.)

Table of Contents:

Dear Student Teacher,

I have prepared this manual to help you through the last and most meaningful stage of your teacher training--student teaching. It is my hope that you will be able to put into practice the theories you have learned, develop techniques of classroom presentation, acquire skills in classroom management, develop rapport with students, and find satisfaction in the fact that you have influenced the academic and personal development of young people.

I assure you that although the task before you is a difficult one, I will always be there to help you through the rough times and applaud your victories. I will not do your work for you, but I will stand behind you as a guide, advisor, counselor, and resource person. Never hesitate to ask for help or advice. My job is to assist you at appropriate opportunities in order to foster the development of your talents and skills.

Expect some challenges; they will bring you growth. Expect some disappointments; they are opportunities for insight and learning. As you proceed, keep me in touch with your feelings and reactions. Perhaps I can give suggestions or clarify something you do not understand. Above all, no matter how it's going, talk to me and allow me to share your experiences or frustrations. I, in turn, promise to do whatever I can to assist you.

I hope that it will become clear to you as you read this manual what I expect of you and what you can expect from me. I have tried to provide clearly defined expectations and goals. We will have periodic and frequent conferences. If there is anything you do not understand, let me know. Finally, I hope that I sound optimistic because I am. I look forward to working with you, endeavoring always to make this a blossoming prelude to your entrance into a successful and fulfilling career.

Sincerely,

My Philosophy of Education:

The premises under which I teach are as follows. The student should:

1. develop the ability to cope with new ideas.

2. experience the satisfaction and self-confidence that comes from mastery of academic studies.

3. learn to grapple with ideas of increasing complexity and increasing degrees of ndependence and creativity.

4. learn to discriminate and not be content with simplistic or prejudicial ideas.

5. acquire a realization of both positive and negative effects of scientific advances upon our world.

My Class Schedule

7:45	Teachers need to be in rooms
8:15	Students may enter classrooms
8:30	Tardy bell for homeroom
8:45	Bell ending homeroom period
8:50–9:40	First period
9:45–10:35	Second period
10:40–11:30	Third period
11:30–12:00	Lunch
12:05–12:55	Fourth period
1:00–1:50	Fifth period
1:55–2:45	Sixth period
2:50–3:40	Seventh period
4:10	Teachers may leave building

My planning period is during fifth period. We will grade papers, discuss plans for the day, plan for future lessons, and meet with other teachers. Although you have no structured duties during this period, you are not permitted to leave the school during this time without knowledge of the principal and me. This is not free time. It is time needed for preparation. You will also help me during hall duty each Monday (8:15–8:30) on the third floor. The dates for late bus duty are on your desk. You are expected to help with this assignment. We shall use the half hour after school each afternoon to discuss your observations, have frequent conferences, and plan laboratory work. Also I want to answer any questions or concerns you may have.

My Expectations from You

1. Be on time. You must be in the classroom one half hour before the students enter the building and remain one half hour after the dismissal bell.

2. Be professional. This means that you respect the authority of your supervisors. It also means that you treat as confidential all matters pertaining to individual students and colleagues. It also requires that you are here to do our best professional work without letting your personal life interfere with classroom performance.

3. Your authority extends over all students in the school. Be alert to disruptions, problems, or misbehaviors in the hall, restrooms, lunchrooms, etc.

4. Have well-defined plans for each lesson that you teach. These plans must be submitted to me at least one day prior to your teaching.

5. Attend all teachers' meetings and parent conferences.

6. Keep an accurate record of attendance in the grade book.

7. Evaluate papers and return them as quickly as possible. Accurately record these grades in the grade book.

8. Keep a thorough record of any necessary disciplinary action taken. Be sure to note the date and the offense. There are various disciplinary forms in your desk. Review these carefully. Give one copy to the student and keep the carbon copy.

9. Bring to my attention and discuss with me the failing performance of any student. Do it early enough so that something can be done.

10. Notify me of any student who is absent or

tardy an excessive number of times.

11. Ask for help when needed. Whether the problem be with discipline, student performance, or your own teaching, let me know before it becomes insurmountable.

12. Help me with any club or, if you wish, help any other teacher if you are interested in any particular club.

13. Do not allow the gossip in the teachers' lounge to affect your attitude toward students. Teachers often "let off steam" and sometimes their information is inaccurate or unfair.

14. Know your material. The students respect you as an authority on the subject. However, do not cover your lack of knowledge by giving incorrect information. It is far better to say "I don't know, but I'll find out.

15. Be in school every day unless you are ill. If there is a legitimate reason for missing discuss it with me prior to the time. Be certain to call me early if you are unable to attend.

What You Can Expect From Me

I will:

1. help you become acquainted with the school, the students, and the administrators and teachers.

2. provide a model of teaching techniques and classroom management.

3. clearly define your duties and responsibilities.

4. help you to become an effective observer.

5. give positive suggestions in writing for improving your teaching performance.

6. supply materials concerning policy, rules, curriculum, lesson planning, etc.

7. answer any questions and discuss any problems you may have.

8. be available at all times, both in and out of school.

9. be a resource, helping you to find further needed curricular materials.

10. give you immediate feedback from my evaluations in verbal and written forms.

11. work with your college supervisor, giving him written records of your progress.

The First Day

The members of the classes have been waiting anxiously to meet you. I will introduce you and encourage you to say a few words about yourself. Allow students to ask you questions and talk to you. This may, perhaps, be done in a structured way by asking each student to give his name and say something about himself. Do whatever seems comfortable to you. First impressions are important.

In the pocket of the front cover of this manual are seating charts for each of the six classes. Use these as you observe today and begin to learn the names of the students as quickly as possible. Knowing names helps to establish rapport and discipline.

You have your own "space" in the room. At the back of the room is a desk where you may keep your materials. I have put the textbooks, student handbook, and a copy of the curriculum in the drawers. This is not your permanent seat! Feel free to move around the class, helping students and getting to know them.

Today during our planning period I will take you on a tour of the school. I will introduce you to our principal, the vice-principals, and several of the teachers.

The First Week

During your first week of student teaching you may want to do the following activities:

1. Continue to learn student names.
2. Become familiar with student interests and needs.
3. Help students with assignments in the laboratory.
4. Help me to set up laboratory experiments.
5. Observe teaching strategies carefully.
6. Become familiar with other teachers.
7. Read the student handbook for school rules and policies.
8. Acquaint yourself with manuals on policy of the state and county. (In the teachers' lounge).
9. Read the booklet in your desk on classroom mangement. Be ready to discuss various disciplinary techniques. Record during your observations the techniques used by me and assess their effectiveness.
10. Study the chemistry and general science curricula as set forth in the state and county guidelines.
11. Become familiar with classroom rules (posted on the bulletin board).
12. Stay for a short while after school to confer about the day's activities.
13. Study the textbooks in your desk. You will have some choices to make about units you would like to teach.

Observation Techniques

During our daily conferences, we will decide what teaching skill or style, student behaviors or responses, or verbal interactions you will observe. As you observe you will need to keep data neat and accurate, with dates recorded. During conferences we will analyze the data.

I have described below some observational techniques. They are written briefly here, but we will discuss them in more detail as we implement their use. I will welcome your input on ideas for observations on any aspect of teaching.

1. <u>Informal and written remarks.</u> Write your impressions of what you see students doing. How are they responding to the teacher? What is your impression of the fectiveness of the lesson?

2. <u>Collecting Data Using a Seating Chart.</u> This technique may be useful in identifying those students who are on task, disruptive, or idle. Select a different group of 5 or 6 students to observe for about five minutes. Keep track of their on or off task behaviors.

3. <u>Analysis of Teacher Performance.</u> Since I am to be your model, you may wish to develop a checklist of my teaching effectiveness. This may help you to notice certain behaviors that you may wish to emulate or disregard. The important thing is that you do not let yourself become a passive observer. Look for specifics and make notes of these.

4. <u>Analysis of Questioning Strategies.</u> Review Bloom's <u>Taxonomy for Questioning Skills.</u> Label each question asked by either student or teacher during the lesson according to its intellectual level: Knowledge, Comprehension, Application, Analysis, Synthesis, Evaluation. Which kinds of questions are asked most frequently? Are all kinds of questions included in the lesson? Make a list of some examples of different kinds of questions that were asked.

5. <u>Observing Classroom Patterns.</u> Make notes or diagrams of the way I move around the

classroom. Do I stay near a certain place in the room or do I cover all areas?

Categories of Exceptional Students

I have placed in your desk a copy of Exceptional Children. Refer to it for more detail in understanding differences in abilities of students. Since our students are mainstreamed you will be working with several of the following types of students.

1. Mentally Impaired
2. Learning Disabled
3. Behavioral Disordered
4. Physically Handicapped
5. Health Impaired
6. Gifted

The following activities may be useful to help you identify special talents, abilities, or problems of the classroom students.

1. Examine permanent records for test scores, grades, or inconsistencies. Study the health records as well.
2. Talk to coaches and attend sporting events if you have student athletes.
3. Attend music and dramatic presentations to discover talents you might be able to enhance.
4. Ask students to write a paragraph about their special interests or hobbies. These exercises may discover students' particular interests as well as abilities to express themselves.
5. Administer simple aptitude tests to determine if certain skills are apparent.
6. Have informal interviews with students to diagnose speech and measure oral verbal skills.
7. Read privately with students to assess their reading and comprehension levels.
8. Learn from grading papers. Look for patterns of errors, continual misspellings, reversals of letters.
9. Use problem solving games with the class and with small groups. Determine qualities of leadership, quick thinking, and group interaction

abilities.

10. Do a sociogram. Allow students to divide into groups for projects with students of their choice.

11. Observe body language. Interpret its meanings for understanding students.

12. Do timed activities to identify those students who are quick and who need more challenging and advanced materials.

The Second and Third Weeks

During these weeks your assignments will change as you have the opportunity to assume more of the teaching responsibilities. When you are not teaching you will continue to observe my class, grade papers, help students, and prepare unit and lesson plans.

While you are teaching I will observe and evaluate your classroom techniques according to the following criteria:

The Lesson
    content objectives
    organization
    materials
    introduction, development, and closure
    promotion of intellectual skills
The Teacher
    attitude
    appearance
    poise and confidence
    knowledge of content
    establishment of a teaching environment
    communication
    flexibility
    recognition and allowances for individual differences
    ability to motivate students
The Student
    behavior
    attentiveness and participation
    achievement and success
    attitudes

Our conferences will become more specific during these two weeks. We will use particular observation techniques to provide as much data as possible. I will be present in the classroom a great deal during this period so that I can provide information and suggestions for you at our conferences.

The Remaining Weeks

After successful conclusion of the third week, I will give you full responsibility for all teaching assignments. If you do not feel ready, we can adopt a part-time schedule. This decision will depend on the development of your skills, confidence, and classroom control. When I leave the room I will let you know where I can be found and a student can come for me if I'm needed by you.

I will observe you periodically and we will have weekly conferences to keep discussing the data and potential improvements. Your specific duites for the final weeks of student teaching will be:

1. submitting weekly lesson plans (to be turned in each Friday) for the following week.
2. designing creative daily plans and unit plans.
3. grading and recording student learning.
4. reporting students who are failing, being tardy, absent, or misbehaving.
5. being responsible for the academic progress, behavior, and safety of students.

Because of the nature of a chemistry class, you have a heavier responsibility than normal for the safety of your students. Make it clear to students that you will tolerate no horseplay or intentional "playing with chemicals." You must be firm on this rule. Always check to see that chemical cupboards are locked, gas jets turned off, and safety glasses worn. There is a list of safety rules posted on the bulletin board. Never conduct a laboratory assignment without pointing out the potential dangers. Check individual set-ups and be alert to unintentional mistakes.

Classroom Rules and Consequences

If the following set of rules are followed a pleasant atmosphere will prevail where the teacher is not forced into the role of policeman or monitor of rules. There also will be less need of long homework assignments since more work will be accomplished in the classroom. Finally improved concentration will result in better learning and improved grades.

1. When the tardy bell rings students must be in their appropriate seats with required materials and pencils ready.
2. Students are not permitted to engage in conversation or actions that are disruptive to the classroom environment.
3. Food, beverages, gum, candy, or tobacco products are not permitted in the classroom.
4. Students must complete all assignments on time and makeup work within two days of an absence unless an extensive period of time has been missed.
5. Cheating will result in a grade of "0."

Consequences for violations of rules 1 to 3:

The first time a student breaks a rule give a conduct grade cut. The second time a student breaks a rule give a conduct grade cut and have a conference with the student. The third time a student breaks a rule include a conduct grade cut and send him to the office. If the offense becomes more serious, the parents of the student must be contacted. Fighting, destruction of property, offensive language or gestures will result in the offending parties being sent to the office immediately.

Daily or Periodic Evaluation

My evaluations of your growth as a teacher will be more frequent at the beginning of the student teaching experience. At first I will be in the classroom all of the time and evaluate you daily. After I leave the classroom, I will appear frequently to evaluate particular aspects of your teaching. We will discuss the focus of the next evaluation at our conferences. You will know what I will be observing and evaluating.

Keep in mind that my subjective comments will be positive and constructive. I will give you freedom in deciding what improvements can be made and how you can make them happen. If you want advice, I will give it. My comments will seek to encourage you to examine areas where positive growth is possible.

The following forms are examples of evaluations. These samples concentrate on certain aspects of teaching. I will use the following rating scale:

1. Superior performance
2. Good job
3. Fair, but needs some improvements
4. Many weaknesses observed
5. Undesirable techniques; changes are necessary

Sample Daily or Periodic Evaluation Forms

A. Focus: Lesson Presentation

--Follows lesson plan
--Lesson is presented clearly
--Meets individual needs
--Projects voice and varies intonation
--Is flexible
--Times activities well

Additional comments:

B. Focus: Classroom Management

--Establishes rapport with students
--Handles minor disruptions well
--Handles major problems effectively
--Is attentive to classroom climate
--Promotes student self-discipline
--Uses fair and consistent consequences to
    misbehaviors

Additional comments:

Final Evaluation

My evaluation of your student teaching will
be based on many ongoing criteria and
observations. Several of the following points
will be considered in the final assessment.

1. Responsibility and reliability
    a. punctuality
    b. attendance
    c. performance of duties and tasks
    d. accuracy and responsiveness in recording
grades and attendance

2. Development of professionalism
    a. cooperative behavior
    b. adherance to rules and policies
    c. appropriate dress and demeanor
    d. confidentiality of appropriate knowledge

3. Teaching effectiveness
    a. classroom management ability
    b. variety of teaching techniques
    c. provision for individual differences in
students
    d. rapport with students
    e. caring attitude toward academic or
personal problems of students
    f. interest and enthusiasm for new ideas
    g. accepting and learning from negative

271

experiences
     h. knowledge of subject matter
     i. quality of presentation skills

General Science Curriculum Yearly Plan

Unit	Title	Length of Time
1.	What is science?	1 week
2.	Science in our world	2 weeks
3.	Scientific measurement	2 weeks
4.	History of science	2 weeks
5.	Great scientists	1 week
6.	Water and pollution	3 weeks
7.	Chemical pollution	2 weeks
8.	Temperature and measurement	2 weeks
9.	Heat phenomena	2 weeks
10.	Wave motion	1 week
11.	Sound	2 weeks
12.	Electricity	2 weeks
13.	Magnetism; Fields	2 weeks
14.	Light	1 week
15.	Atomic structure	1 week
16.	The periodic table	1 week
17.	The solar system	3 weeks
18.	The planet Earth	3 weeks
19.	Individual projects	1 week
20.	Review and evaluation	2 weeks

                                          36 weeks

Sample Daily Lesson Plan (The Atmosphere)

Objectives:
 1. Explain why the atmosphere is essential to life.
 2. Describe the nature of the atmosphere.
 3. Define the term "atmospheric pressure" and describe the manner in which it is measured.
 4. List the components of the air.

Procedure:

1. Lecture (20 minutes)
 Why we need the atmosphere
  --elements necessary to life
  --protective nature
 The atmospheric layer
  --troposhere
  --stratosphere
  --ionosphere
 Air pressure
  --definition
  --how measured
 The composition of the air
  --elements
  --water vapor

2. Demonstration (10 minutes)

 Using a vacuum pump, remove the air from a metal can. Discuss possible reasons for this phenomenon.

3. Discussion and question/answer session (10 minutes)

 Questions for reinforcement and discussion:
 --What is the atmosphere?
 --Of what is it composed?
 --Why is the atmosphere layered?
 --Why do we need the atmosphere?
 --What is the most abundant element of the air? the least abundant?

273

--What is the most important element?

--Why would you not define the atmosphere as a solution?

4. Closure (5-10 minutes)

Discuss what modern pollution is doing to the atmosphere. Give challenging take home assignment.

About The Authors

Pamela M. Balch is an Associate Professor in Education and Director of the Graduate Program at West Virginia Wesleyan College and instructs education majors, graduate students, and works with cooperating teachers. She has seven years of elementary teaching and supervising experience. Dr. Balch is the author of several journal articles, research studies, and higher education law reviews.

Patrick Balch is an Associate Professor of Science Education at West Virginia University, teaches science methods courses, and supervises student teachers. He has twelve years of teaching, administering, and supervising experience at the secondary level at Yuba City, CA. He also has co-authored several science textbooks and teacher education films. He was a consultant and writer for Biological Sciences Curriculum Study and currently is co-authoring Inter-Science, a three textbook science curriculum for the middle school.